Alexander Grant

Aristotle

Alexander Grant

Aristotle

ISBN/EAN: 9783337006716

Printed in Europe, USA, Canada, Australia, Japan

Cover: Foto ©Thomas Meinert / pixelio.de

More available books at **www.hansebooks.com**

BY

SIR ALEXANDER GRANT, BART., LL.D.
PRINCIPAL OF THE UNIVERSITY OF EDINBURGH

WILLIAM BLACKWOOD AND SONS
EDINBURGH AND LONDON
1898

CONTENTS.

		PAGE
CHAP. I.	THE LIFE OF ARISTOTLE,	1
,, II.	THE WORKS OF ARISTOTLE,	30
,, III.	THE 'ORGANON' OF ARISTOTLE,	50
,, IV.	ARISTOTLE'S 'RHETORIC' AND 'ART OF POETRY,'	77
,, V.	ARISTOTLE'S 'ETHICS,'	100
,, VI.	ARISTOTLE'S 'POLITICS,'	117
,, VII.	THE NATURAL PHILOSOPHY OF ARISTOTLE,	130
,, VIII.	THE BIOLOGY OF ARISTOTLE,	146
,, IX.	THE METAPHYSICS OF ARISTOTLE,	161
,, X.	ARISTOTLE SINCE THE CHRISTIAN ERA,	179

ARISTOTLE.

CHAPTER I.

THE LIFE OF ARISTOTLE.

The dates of the chief events in the life of Aristotle, extracted from the 'Chronology' of Apollodorus (140 B.C.), have been handed down to us by Diogenes Laertius in his 'Lives of the Philosophers;' and from various other sources it is possible to fill in the outline thus afforded, if not with certain facts, at all events with reasonable probabilities. Aristotle's own writings are almost entirely devoid of personal references, yet in them we can trace, to some extent, the progress and development of his mind. On the whole, we know quite as much about him, personally, as about most of the ancient Greek writers.

Aristotle was born in the year 384 B.C., at Stageira, a Grecian colony and seaport town on the Strymonic Gulf in Thrace, not far from Mount Athos—and, what is more important, not far from the frontier of Macedonia, and from Pella, the residence of the Macedonian

King Amyntas. To Stageira, his birth-place, he owed the world-famous appellation of "the Stagirite," given to him by scholiasts and schoolmen in later days. It was fancied by Wilhelm von Humboldt that Aristotle exhibits certain un-Greek characteristics in his neglect of form and grace in writing, and that this is attributable to his having been born and brought up in Thrace. But, on the other hand, Aristotle's family were purely Hellenic, and probably the colonists of Stageira lived in strict conformity with Greek ideas, and not without contempt for the surrounding "barbarians." Even the court of Macedonia, in the neighbourhood, were phil-Hellenic in their tastes, and entertained Greek artists and men of letters. And Aristotle shows no trace in his writings of ever having known any language beside Greek. Probably the mere locality of his birth produced but little influence upon him, except so far as it led to his subsequent connection with the court of Macedon. His father, Nicomachus, was physician to King Amyntas, and it is possible that the youthful Aristotle was taken at times to the court, and thus made the acquaintance of his future patron, Philip of Macedon, who was about his own age. But all through the time of Aristotle's boyhood, affairs in Macedonia were troubled and unprosperous. Amyntas was an unsuccessful ruler, and brought his country to the verge of extinction in a war with the Illyrians. Aristotle, as a youth, cannot have had any inducement to take an interest in Macedonian politics. Up to the time when he left his native city, there had appeared no indication of that which afterwards occurred,—that

Macedonia would conquer the East, and become the mistress of the entire liberties of Greece.

But there is one significant tradition about Aristotle which suggests circumstances likely to have produced in early life a considerable influence upon his habits and pursuits. His father is said to have been an "Asclepiad,"—that is, he belonged to that distinguished caste who claimed to be the descendants of Esculapius. Now we have it, on the authority of Galen,* that "it was the custom in Asclepiad families for the boys to be trained by their father in the practice of dissection, just as regularly as boys in other families learn to read and write." If Aristotle had really been trained from boyhood in the manner thus described, we can understand how great an impulse he would have received to those physiological researches which formed so important a part of his subsequent achievements. But in one place of his writings ('On the Parts of Animals,' I. v. 7), he speaks of the "extreme repugnance" with which one necessarily sees "veins, and flesh, and other suchlike parts," in the human subject. This does not show the hardihood of a practised dissector. But Aristotle's youthful dissections, if made at all, were doubtless made on the lower animals. At all events, we may perhaps safely conclude about him, that he received from his father an hereditary tendency towards physiological study. But in addition to this tendency, Aristotle must doubtless have early manifested an interest in, and capacity for, abstract philosophy.

We now come to the second epoch in his life. About

* Quoted by Grote, 'Aristotle,' i. 4.

the year 367 B.C., when he was seventeen years old, his father having recently died, he was sent by his guardian, Proxenus of Atarneus, to complete his studies at Athens, "the metropolis of wisdom."* There he continued to reside for twenty years, during the greater part of which time he attended the school of philosophy which Plato had founded in the olive-groves of Academus, on the banks of the Cephisus. He had probably inherited from his father means sufficient for his support, so that he could live without care for the acquirement of anything save knowledge. But in the acquisition of this he manifested a zeal unsurpassed in the annals of study. Among his fellow-pupils in the Academe, he is said to have got the *sobriquet* of "the Reader;" while Plato himself called him "the Mind of the School," in recognition of his quick and powerful intelligence. In order to win time, even from sleep, Aristotle is said to have invented the plan of sleeping with a ball in his hand, so held over a brazen dish, that whenever his grasp relaxed the ball would descend with a clang, and arouse him to the resumption of his labours.

Plato's philosophy was absolutely pre-eminent in Greece at this time. It embodied within itself all that was best in the doctrine and the spirit of Socrates, and beyond it there was nothing, except the mystical theories of the Pythagoreans (the best elements in which Plato had assimilated), and the materialistic theories of the Atomists, which Plato, and afterwards Aristotle, controverted. The writings of Aristotle are quite consistent with the tradition that he was for twenty years

* Plato, 'Protagoras,' p. 337. Professor Jowett's translation.

a pupil of the Academic school. They show a long list of thoughts and expressions borrowed from the works of Plato, and also not unfrequently refer to the oral teaching of Plato. They contain a logical, ethical, political, and metaphysical philosophy, which is evidently, with some modifications, the organisation and development of rich materials often rather suggested than worked out in the Platonic dialogues. Aristotle thus, in constructing a system of knowledge which was destined immensely to influence the thoughts of mankind, became, in the first place, the disciple of Plato and the intellectual heir of Socrates; and summed up all the best that had been arrived at by the previous philosophers of Greece.

The personal relationships which arose between Aristotle and his master Plato have furnished matter for uncertain traditions and for much discussion. There seems, however, to be no ground for sustaining the charge of "ingratitude" against Aristotle. The truth was probably somewhat as follows: Aristotle, while engaged in imbibing deeply the philosophical thoughts of Plato, gradually developed also his own individuality and independence of mind. And the natural bias of his intellect was certainly in a different direction from that of Plato. It has been said that "every man is born either a Platonist or an Aristotelian;" and it would be very fortunate if that were literally true, for then every man would be born with a noble type of intellect. But it is no doubt correct to say that the Platonic and the Aristotelian type of intellect are distinct and divergent. They have in common the keen and unwearied pressure after truth, but they seek the truth under different aspects. Plato was ever aspiring to intuitions of a truth which in this world could never be wholly revealed, — a truth of which glimpses only could be obtained, partly by the most abstract powers of thought, partly by the imagination. While richly endowed with humour and the dramatic faculty, and the most trenchant insight into the fallacies of mankind, Plato was not content with aiming at those demonstrations which could be stated once for all, but he rather sought analogies and hints of a truth which can never be definitely expressed. Eternity, the life of the gods, the supra-sensible world of "pure ideas," were of more reality and importance to him than the affairs of this life. While he was the greatest and most original of metaphysical philosophers, he never ceased to be a poet, and, to some extent, a mystic.

The intellectual characteristics of Aristotle, as known to us from his works, present a great contrast to all this. He was too much in earnest, and at the same time too matter-of-fact, to allow poetry and the imagination any share in the quest for truth. He had no taste for half-lights; and with regard to such great questions as the immortality of the soul, the nature of God, the operation of Providence, and the like, it is evident that so far from preferring these, he rather kept aloof from them, and only gave cautious and grudging utterances upon them. His passion was for definite knowledge, especially knowledge so methodised that it could be stated in the form of a general principle, or law. He thought that to obtain a general principle in which knowledge was summed up, on any subject, was of the utmost importance ;* that such a principle was a possession for all future time, that future generations would apply to it and work it out in detail, and thus that it would form the nucleus of a science. And this was the daring aim of Aristotle—no less than the foundation of all the sciences. We shall have occasion to point out subsequently the imperfections of Aristotle's method in physical science when compared with that of modern times. But for all that, his spirit was essentially scientific, and for the sake of science and the naked truth he discarded all beauty and grace of style. Plato on the other hand was an artist, and clothed all his thoughts in beauty; and if there be (as there surely is) † a truth which is above the truth of scientific knowledge, that was the truth after which Plato aspired. Aristotle's aspirations were for methodised experience and the definite.

It is easy to understand, or imagine, how two great minds with such divergent tendencies would be unable to continue for ever to stand to each other in the relation of pupil to teacher. For a time, no doubt, the divergence would not be discovered. Aristotle at first would appear only as "the mind" of Plato's school. And his first attempts at philosophical writing appear to have been made in the form of dialogues in somewhat feeble imitation of the masterpieces of Plato. We shall speak hereafter of this early and lighter class of Aristotle's writings. He may have adhered for

* See 'Soph. Elench.' xxxii. 13 ; 'Eth.' I. vii. 17-21.
† See Lotze's 'Microcosmus,' Einleitung.

several years to this mode of composition. But all the while his powers, his knowledge, and his methods of thought were maturing, and he was working his way to the conception of a quite different mode of setting forth philosophy. Gradually, as he grasped, or thought he had grasped, all that Plato had to impart, his mind would tend to dwell more on those aspects of Plato's thought with which he did not sympathise. He would especially feel a sort of impatience at the licence allowed to the imagination to intrude itself into the treatment of philosophic questions,—at the substitution of gorgeous myths and symbolical figures for plain exact answers of the understanding. This feeling of impatience broke out in a polemic against that doctrine of the eternal " Ideas " or Forms of Things, which appears somewhat variously set forth in Plato's dialogues, especially in 'Timæus,' 'Phædrus,' and 'Republic,' and which doubtless formed a prominent topic in Plato's discourses to his school. We are told by Proclus* that Aristotle " proclaimed loudly in his dialogues that he was unable to sympathise with the doctrine of Ideas, even though his opposition to it should be attributed to a factious spirit." The import of that doctrine was to disparage the world of sensible objects. It represented that when we, by means of our senses, apprehend, or think that we apprehend, particular objects, we are like men sitting in a dimly-lighted subterranean cavern, and staring at shadows on the wall; that the world of sense is a world of shadows, but that a true world exists,—a world of Ideas; that

* Quoted by Philoponus, ii. 2.

nothing is really good or beautiful in the world of sense, but what we call good or beautiful things are those which have a faint semblance to the Idea of the good or the beautiful, and thus bring back to our souls the remembrance of those Ideas, which we once saw in our ante-natal condition; that the Ideas or Forms are archetypes, in accordance with which the Creator framed this world; that they are not only the cause of qualities and attributes in things, such as goodness, justice, equality, and the like, but also they are heads of classes or universals, and that they alone have complete reality, while the individuals, constituting the classes at the head of which they stand, only "participate" to a certain extent in real existence. Such were some of the features of Plato's celebrated doctrine of Ideas. That he did not himself hold very strongly or dogmatically to its details, may be judged from the fact that in two of his dialogues ('Parmenides' and 'Sophist') he himself points out, and does not remove, many difficulties which attach to them. But the main gist of the doctrine was to assert what is called Realism; and this, under one form or another, Plato always maintained. When Aristotle attacked the doctrine of Ideas, there was the first beginning of that controversy between the Realists and the Nominalists, which so much excited the minds of men in the middle ages. Realism, making reason independent of the senses, asserts that the universal is more real than the particular,—that, for instance, the universal idea of "man" in general is more real, and can be grasped by the mind with greater certainty, than the conception of any individual man. Nominalism, on the contrary, asserts the superior reality of individual objects, and turns the universal into a mere name. Now it was quite natural for Aristotle, with his tendency towards physical science and experiment, and the amassing of particular facts, to take the Nominalist view, so far as to assert the reality of individual objects. But there is reason for doubting that he ever became a thorough and consistent Nominalist. For the present it is sufficient to note that at the outset of his philosophical career he appears to have made an onslaught, in several dialogues which he wrote for the purpose, on Plato's doctrine of Ideas. In three passages of his extant works ('Eth.' I. vi.; 'Met.' I. vi., XII. iv.), he gives summaries of his arguments on the subject. He couches those arguments in courteous language, and in one place introduces them with words which have been Latinised into the well-known phrase —*Amicus Plato, sed magis amica Veritas.* Yet the arguments themselves appear somewhat captious. And there may have been a youthful vehemence in the mode in which he first urged them. Here probably first appeared "the little rift within the lute;" this was the beginning of that divergence of mind and attitude which, growing wider, rendered it ultimately impossible that Aristotle should be chosen to succeed Plato, as inheritor of his method, and head of the Academic school.

In another set of circumstances, tradition affords us indications of the independence and self-confidence of Aristotle having been manifested during the lifetime of

Plato. In his extant writings, Plato speaks so disparagingly of the art of Rhetoric, that we can hardly fancy his giving any encouragement to the study of it among his disciples. But none the less Aristotle appears to have diligently laboured in this, as in every other intellectual province that he found open. Plato would not separate Rhetoric from the rhetorical spirit; he regarded the whole thing as a procedure for tickling the ears, for flattering crowds, for subordinating truth to effect. Aristotle, in the analytical way which became one of his chief characteristics, separated the method of Rhetoric from the uses to which it might be applied. He saw that success in Rhetoric depended on general principles and laws of the human mind, and that it would be worth while to draw these out and frame them into a science, especially as many of his countrymen had already essayed to do the same, though imperfectly. He maintained that the study of the methods of Rhetoric was desirable and even necessary to a free citizen, for self-defence, for the exposure of sophistry, and in the interests of truth itself. Now, the greatest school of Rhetoric in all Greece was at this period held in Athens by the renowned Isocrates, who, when Aristotle arrived at Athens, was at the zenith of his reputation. He was now nearly seventy years old, but continued to teach and to compose with almost unabated vigour for twenty-eight years more. Isocrates had been the follower of Socrates, and several leading Sophists of the latter part of the fifth century B.C.—Protagoras, Prodicus, Gorgias, and Theramenes—are named as having been his teachers.* He was a dignified old man, full of the most elevated sentiments. The style of his oratory had been formed after the florid Sicilian school of Gorgias, but was more severe and artistic than the earlier models of that school. He professed to inculcate what he called "philosophy," but which was really a kind of thought standing half-way between pure speculative search for truth, like that of Plato, and the merely worldly and practical aims of the Sophists. It was a manly wisdom dealing with politics and morality, analogous to the reflections on such subjects in which Cicero afterwards indulged. The rhetorical school of Isocrates drew pupils from all parts of Greece, from Sicily, and even from Pontus. In it, says Cicero, "the eloquence of all Greece was trained and perfected." The pupils remained in it sometimes three or four years; they paid a fee of 1000 drachmæ each (= 1000 francs, or £40); and thus in his long life the master became one of the most opulent citizens of Athens. "Isocrates," says Dionysus, "had the educating of the best of the youth of Greece," and so many of his scholars became afterwards distinguished in various ways—as orators, statesmen, generals, historians, or philosophers—that a list of them was drawn up by Hermippus. Among the number was Speusippus, nephew to Plato, and afterwards his successor in the headship of the Academy. And yet it may readily be believed that there was small sympathy between the Academy and the school of Isocrates,

---

* See Professor Jebb's 'Attic Orators from Antiphon to Isæos,' ii. 5.

the aims of the two being so very different. Plato and his followers looked down with more or less contempt on the half-philosophising of Isocrates. And at last the youthful Aristotle came forward as a champion, challenging and attacking the highly-reputed veteran. Aristotle is said to have parodied on this occasion a line of Euripides—

> "What! must I
> In silence leave barbarians to speak?
> Never!"

and to have taken for his motto the words—

> "What? must I
> In silence leave Isocrates to speak?"

The acrimony of the allusion suggests to us the spirit in which he opened the controversy. He seems to have assailed the matter of the discourses of Isocrates, as being of a superficial and merely oratorical character, and also his theory of the art of rhetoric, and his mode of teaching it. The strictures of Aristotle were answered by Cephisodorus, one of the pupils of Isocrates, who wrote a defence of his master in four books. Both attack and reply have completely perished. Aristotle appears to have followed up his theoretical denunciation of Isocrates by the practical step of opening a school of Rhetoric in rivalry to his. What the success of this enterprise may have been is not recorded. There is no reason for supposing that the young Stagirite at all succeeded in impressing the Athenians at that time with his superior insight into the laws of Rhetoric. The real value and scientific pre-eminence of his views came out in the immortal treatise on Rhetoric, which many years later he composed. But it is remarkable that that treatise, while full of references to Isocrates, bears no traces of any ill-feeling towards him. In fact, it would seem that time must have worked a certain change in the character of Aristotle, for almost the only glimpses which we have of him during his earlier residence at Athens show him somewhat petulantly attacking both Plato and Isocrates; whereas his works which we possess, and which were written later, are calmly impersonal and devoid of all petulance of spirit.

Plato died in the year 347 B.C., and we find that in that year Aristotle, together with his fellow-disciple Xenocrates, left Athens, and went to reside at Atarneus, a town of Asia Minor. This migration was doubtless caused by the choice of Speusippus, Plato's nephew, to be Leader of the Academy. However natural it may have been that Aristotle should be held disqualified by incompatibility of opinions for becoming the representative of Plato, still it may have been unpleasant to him to see another preferred to himself, and especially one so inferior to himself in intellect as Speusippus. And Xenocrates may have felt something of the same kind on his own account. Accordingly, the two left Athens together. Aristotle had more than one reason for selecting Atarneus as his new place of abode. It was the home of Proxenus, his guardian, of whom mention has already been made; and it was ruled over by Hermeias, an enlightened prince, with whom both Aristotle and Xenocrates had had the opportunity of forming a philosophic friendship. The history of Hermeias was remarkable: he had been the slave of Eubulus, the former despot of Atarneus. As happens not uncommonly in the East, he had sprung from being slave to be vizier, and thence to be ruler himself. He governed beneficently; and, his mind not being devoid of philosophical impulses, he had come to Athens and attended the lectures of Plato. He now hospitably received the two emigrants from Plato's school, and entertained them at his court for three years, during which time he bestowed the hand of Pythias, his niece, upon Aristotle in marriage. This may be conceived to have been a happy period of Aristotle's life, but it was cut short by the death of his benefactor, who was treacherously kidnapped by a Greek officer in the service of the Persians, and put to death. Aristotle afterwards recorded his admiration for Hermeias, in a hymn or pæan which he wrote in his honour, and in which he likened him to Hercules and the Dioscuri, and other heroes of noble endurance. He also perhaps alludes to him in a well-known passage* in which he says that "a good man does not become a friend to one who is in a superior station to himself, unless that superiority of station be justified by superiority of merit." If Aristotle had Hermeias, his own former friend, in his mind when he wrote this passage, he must have generously attributed to him moral qualities superior to his own.

On flying from Atarneus, as they were now obliged to do, Xenocrates returned to Athens, and Aristotle

* 'Ethics,' VIII. vi. 6.

took up his abode with his wife at Mitylene, where he lived two or three years, until he was invited by Philip of Macedon to become the tutor of Alexander, then a boy of the age of thirteen. That Aristotle, the prince of philosophers and supreme master of the sphere of knowledge, should be called upon to train the mind of Alexander, the conqueror of the world, seems a combination so romantic, that it has come to be thought that it must have been the mere invention of some sophist or rhetorician. This, however, is an unnecessary scepticism, for antiquity is unanimous in accepting the tradition, and there are no circumstances that we know of which are inconsistent with it. Aristotle's family connection with the royal family of Macedon made it natural that now, when he had acquired a certain reputation in Greece, he should be offered this charge. Unfortunately no information has been handed down to us as to the way in which he performed its duties. History is silent on the subject, and we cannot even gather from any of Aristotle's own writings his views as to the education of a prince; the treatise on education, which was to have formed part of his 'Politics,' has reached us as an incomplete or mutilated fragment. Nothing that is recorded of Alexander tends to throw any light on his early training, except, perhaps, his interest in Homer and in the Attic tragedians, and his power of addressing audiences in Greek, which was, of course, to a Macedonian an acquired language. It is reasonable to suppose that Aristotle instructed him in rhetoric, and imbued him with Greek literature, and took him through a course of mathematics. Whether he attempted anything beyond this "secondary instruction" we know not. But it would be vain to look for traces of a personal and intellectual influence having been produced by the teacher on the mind of his pupil. Alexander's was a genius of that first-rate order that grows independently of, or soon outgrows, all education. His mind was not framed to be greatly interested in science or philosophy; he was, as the First Napoleon said of himself, *tout à fait un être politique;* and even during part of the period of Aristotle's tutelage, he was associated with his father in the business of the State. On the whole, we might almost imagine that Aristotle's functions at the court of Macedonia were light, and that he was allowed considerable leisure for the quiet prosecution of his own great undertakings. He seems, however, to have enjoyed the full confidence and favour of his patrons,* and to have retained his appointment altogether about five years, until Philip was assassinated in the year 336 B.C., and Alexander became King of Macedonia.

For a year after the death of Philip, Aristotle still remained, residing either at Pella or at Stageira; but of course no longer as preceptor to Alexander, whose mind was now totally absorbed by imperial business and plans for the subjugation of all the peoples of the

* Aristotle at this time obtained the permission of Philip to rebuild and resettle his native city, Stageira, which had been sacked and ruined in the Olynthian war (349-347 B.C.) He collected the citizens, who had been scattered abroad, invited new comers, and made laws for the community. In memory of these services an annual festival was afterwards held in his honour at Stageira.

East,—while his own mind was meditating plans different in kind, but no less vast, for the subjugation of all the various realms of knowledge. In 335 B.C., the preparations for Alexander's oriental campaigns were commenced in earnest, and Aristotle then again betook himself, after a twelve years' absence, to Athens, whither he returned with all the prestige which could be derived from the most marked indications of the favour of Alexander, who ordered a statue of him to be set up at Athens, and who is said also to have furnished him with ample funds for the prosecution of physical and zoological investigations. Athenæus computes the total sum given to Aristotle in that way at 800 talents (nearly £200,000); and, if this had been the actual fact, it would have been, perhaps, the greatest instance on record of the "endowment of research." But we can only treat the statement as at best mere hearsay. We know how amounts of this kind are invariably exaggerated; and, indeed, the whole story may have arisen from the imagination of later Greek writers dwelling on the relationship between the philosopher and the king. The same may be said of Pliny's assertion, that "thousands of men" in Alexander's army were put at the orders of Aristotle for the purposes of scientific inquiry and collection. Had this been true, Aristotle, though far from being able to make the use which now would be made of such an opportunity, would have been in a position which many a biologist of the present day might envy. Even discounting all such statements as uncertain and questionable, we must still admit that Aristotle, in his 50th year, was enabled, under the most favourable auspices, to commence building up the great fabric of philosophy and science for which he had been, all his life long, making the plans and gathering the materials.

Aristotle, on his return, found Speusippus dead, and Xenocrates installed as leader of the Platonic school of Philosophy, which was held, as we have said, in the groves of Academe, on the west of the city of Athens. He immediately opened a rival school on the eastern side, in the grounds attached to the Temple of the Lyceian Apollo. From his using the covered walks (*peripatoi*) in these grounds for lecturing to, and intercourse with, his pupils, the name of "Peripatetics" came to be given to his scholars, and to the Aristotelian sect in general. His object being research, and the bringing into methodised form the results of investigations,—it may be asked why he should have opened a school? Partly, this was necessitated by a regard for his own reputation and fame,—it was a method of publication suitable before the days of printing. And also in many ways it could be made to further his views. Teaching a philosophical school was a very different thing from teaching the rudiments. It was more like the work of a German professor, who often does not condescend to impart anything to his class, except his own latest discoveries. The very practice of imparting to an auditory reasoned-out conclusions is a stimulus to their production, and at the same time a test of their correctness. Thus, Aristotle, in his writings, frequently uses the term "teaching" merely to indicate "demonstration;" and as there is reason to believe that all his great works were written at this time, we may conceive, with great likelihood, that all the "demonstrations" they contain had at one time the form of "teachings"—that is to say, that they went through the process of being read to his school. But there was another special way in which Aristotle was able not only to benefit his scholars, but also to make use of them as subordinate labourers in his work. We must remember what he was aiming at: it was to produce what we should call an encyclopædia of all the sciences. Such a book, nowadays, is done by many different hands, and the different articles in it do not aim at being original, but at compiling the latest results of the best authorities in each department. But Aristotle sought to construct an encyclopædia with his own hand, in which each science should appear brand-new, originally created or quite reconstructed by himself. He began from the very beginning, and framed his own philosophical or scientific nomenclature; he traced out the laws on which human reasoning proceeds, and was the first to reduce these to science, and to produce a Logic. He wrote anew 'Metaphysics,' 'Ethics,' 'Politics,' 'Rhetoric,' and 'The Art of Poetry;' and while these were still on the stocks, he was engaged in founding, on the largest scale, the physical and natural sciences, especially natural philosophy, physiology under various aspects (such as histology and anatomy, embryology, psychology, the philosophy of the senses, &c.), and, above all, natural history. Much of this work, especially its more abstract part, was the slowly-ripened fruit of his entire previous life. But though he had great stores ready that only required to be arranged and put forth, he never ceased pushing out inquiries in all directions, and collecting fresh materials. He had quite the Baconian zeal for *experientia tabulata*, for lists and memoranda of all kinds of facts, historical, political, psychological, or naturalistic. He loved to note problems to be solved and difficulties to be answered. Thus a boundless field of subordinate labour was opened, in which his pupils might be employed. The absence of any effort after artistic beauty in his writings made it easier to incorporate here and there the contributions of his apprentices. And his works, as we have them, exhibit some traces of co-operative work. The Peripatetic school, after his death, followed the direction which Aristotle had given them, and were noted for their monographs on small particular points.

Aristotle was not a citizen of Athens, but only a "metic," or foreign resident, so he took no part in public affairs. His whole time during the thirteen years of his second residence in the city—a period coeval with the astonishing career of Alexander in the East—must have been devoted to labours within his school, especially in connection with the composition of his works. From the enthusiastic passages in which he speaks of the joys of the philosopher, we may conceive how highly the privileges of this period—so calm and yet so intensely active—were appreciated by him. But few traditions bearing upon this part of his life have been handed down. These chiefly point to his relations with Alexander, with whom, as well as with

Antipater, who was acting as viceroy in Macedonia, he is represented as having maintained a friendly correspondence. Cassander, the son of Antipater, appears to have attended his school. As time went on, the character of Alexander became corrupted * by unchecked success, Asiatic influences, and the all but universal servility which he encountered. His mind became alienated from those Greek citizens around him who showed any independence of spirit. He quarrelled with Antipater, who was faithfully acting for him at home. On a frivolous charge he cruelly put to death Callisthenes, a young orator whom, on the recommendation of Aristotle, he had taken in his retinue. On this and other occasions he is said to have broken out into bitter expressions against "the sophistries" of Aristotle,—that is to say, his free and reasonable political principles. The East, conquered physically by Alexander, had conquered and changed the mind of its conqueror. And he had now fallen quite out of sympathy with his ancient preceptor and friend. But the Athenians seem to have been unconscious of any such change. Aristotle had come to Athens as the avowed favourite and *protégé* of Alexander, and that, too, at a moment when Alexander (335 B.C.), by sacking the city of Thebes, and by compelling Athens with the threat of a similar fate to exile some of her anti-Macedonian statesmen, had made himself the object of sullen dread and covert dislike to the majority of the Athenian citizens. Some portion of this feeling was doubtless reflected upon Aristotle, but during the life of Alexander

* See Grote's 'History of Greece,' xii. 291, 301, 341.

any manifestation of it was checked, the affairs of Athens being administered for the time by the "Macedonian" party. Of this party Aristotle was naturally regarded as a pronounced adherent, and he came even to be identified with those arbitrary and tyrannical acts of Alexander, which must in reality have been most repugnant to him. This was especially the case in 324 B.C., when Alexander thought fit to insult the Hellenic cities, by sending a proclamation to be read by a herald at the Olympic Games, ordering them to recall all citizens who were under sentence of banishment, and threatening with instant invasion any city which should hesitate to obey this command. The officer charged with bearing this offensive proclamation, so galling to the self-respect of the Grecian communities, turned out to be none other than Nicanor of Stageira, son of Proxenus the guardian of Aristotle, and now the ward and destined son-in-law of Aristotle himself. This unfortunate circumstance could not fail to draw upon the philosopher, without any fault of his own, the animosity of the Athenian people. In the summer of the next year (323 B.C.), the eyes of all Greece were still anxiously fixed upon the movements of Alexander, when of a sudden the startling news thrilled through every city that the life of the great conqueror had been cut short by a violent fever at Babylon. The news caused a sensation throughout the states of Greece analogous to what would have been felt throughout Europe had Napoleon been suddenly cut off, say in the year 1810.

By the death of Alexander the position of Aristotle

at Athens was profoundly affected. The anti-Macedonian party at once, for the moment, regained power; the statesmen who had hitherto protected him were forced to fly from the city, and the spirit of reaction included him also in its attacks. It now became clear that Aristotle had a host of enemies in Athens. There were three classes of persons from whom especially these hostile ranks would naturally be recruited: 1st, The numerous friends of the orator Isocrates, with whom Aristotle in earlier life had put himself in competition; 2d, The Platonists, who resented Aristotle's divergence from their master and his polemic against certain points of the Platonic system; 3d, The anti-Macedonian party, who indiscriminately visited on Aristotle the political acts of Alexander. Feelings that had been long repressed and kept concealed, while Aristotle was strong in political support, were now licensed by the changed circumstances to come forth into act. His enemies seized on the moment to do him a mischief. An indictment, charging him with "impiety," was drawn up by Eurymedon, the chief priest of the Eleusinian Ceres, aided by a son of Ephorus, the historian, who had been one of the pupils of Isocrates. Matter for this accusation was obtained partly from Aristotle's poem written in honour of Hermeias, and which equalled him to the demi-gods, partly from the fact that Aristotle had placed a statue of Hermeias in the temple at Delphi, partly also from some passages in his published writings which were pointed to as inconsistent with the national religion. A philosopher's view must necessarily differ from the popular view of the topics of religion. Yet in his extant works Aristotle is always tender and reverent in dealing with popular beliefs; indeed, in modern times, these works have been regarded as a bulwark of ecclesiastical feeling. The whole charge, if taken on its real merits, must be considered utterly frivolous; yet those who would have to try the case—a large jury taken from the general mass of the citizens—could not be depended on for discrimination in such a question. They would be too subject to the currents of envy, political, personal, and anti-philosophical, setting in from various quarters; they would be too readily imbued with the *odium theologicum*. Nothing but a very general popularity would have been an effectual protection at such a moment, and this it is not likely that Aristotle ever possessed in Athens. While capable of devoted and generous friendship, he may easily have been cold and reserved towards general society. He was absorbed in study, and probably lived confined within the narrow scientific circle of his own school. He may even have exhibited some of those proud characteristics which he attributes in his 'Ethics' to the "great-souled" man, "who claims great things for himself because he is worthy of them," and "who cannot bear to associate with any one except a friend." However this may have been, he was probably right on the present occasion to decline submitting his life and opinions to the judgment of the populace of Athens. He availed himself of the law which gave to any accused person the option of quitting the city before the day of trial, and he retired to Chalcis in Eubœa, "in order," as he is reported to have said, "that the Athenians might not have another opportunity of sinning against philosophy, as they had already done once in the person of Socrates."

Chalcis was the original home of the ancestry of Aristotle, and he appears to have had some property there; but it was especially a safe place of refuge for him, as being occupied at this time by a Macedonian garrison. He probably intended only to make a short sojourn there, till circumstances should be changed. He must have fully foreseen that in a short space of time the Macedonian arms would prevail, and restore at Athens the government which had hitherto protected him. He left his school and library in charge of Theophrastus, doubtless looking forward to a speedy return to them and to the resumption of those labours which had already consummated so much. And all this would have happened but that, within a year's time, in 322 B.C., he was seized with illness, and died somewhat suddenly at Chalcis, in the sixty-third year of his age. The story that he had taken poison may be dismissed as fabulous. A more trustworthy account speaks of his having suffered from impaired digestion, the natural result of his habits of application, and this may very likely have been the cause of his death.

The will of Aristotle, or what professes to be such, has been preserved amongst a heap of very questionable traditions, by Diogenes Laertius. If not genuine it is cleverly invented, and is the work of a romancer who wished to credit the Stagirite with evidences of a generous and just disposition. The property to be disposed of seems considerable, analogous perhaps to an estate of £50,000 in the present day. The chief beneficiary under the will is Nicanor (before mentioned), whom Aristotle appoints to marry Pythias, — his daughter by the niece of Hermeias,—so soon as she shall be of marriageable age. Aristotle's first wife had died, and he had subsequently married Herpyllis of Stageira, who became the mother of his son Nicomachus. The will places Nicomachus under the care of Nicanor, and makes liberal provision for Herpyllis, who is mentioned in terms of affection and gratitude. Several of the slaves are thought of, and are to be presented with money and set at liberty; all the young slaves are to be freed, " if they deserve it," as soon as they are grown up. Nicanor is charged to transfer the bones of Aristotle's first wife Pythias to his own place of interment, to provide and dedicate suitable busts of various members of Aristotle's family, and to fulfil a vow formerly made by himself of four marble figures of animals to Zeus the Preserver and Athene the Preserver. This last clause throws suspicion on the genuineness of the document, for it looks like a mere imitation of the dying injunction of Socrates : "We owe a cock to Æsculapius; pay the debt and do not fail." Other points also suggest doubt : for instance, Antipater is named as chief executor, and this detail has the appearance of being the work of a forger availing himself of a well-known name; again, there is a difficulty about Pythias the daughter of Aristotle being too young for marriage at the time of her father's death,—he had married her mother some twenty-three years previously, and had been subsequently married. The terms of the will would imply that Nicomachus was a mere child when his father died, which is inconsistent with other considerations. These and other points of criticism which might be urged do not absolutely prove the will to have been a forgery, they only leave us in doubt about it. And, as has been said, even if regarded as a mere fabrication, it is still a tribute of antiquity to the virtue of Aristotle.

On the other hand, this great name did not escape without incurring its full share of carping and detractation. And the gossip-mongers of the later Roman empire, including Fathers of the Church, have handed on some of the hearsay reports, smart sayings of epigrammatists, and attacks of hostile schools of philosophy, which had been levelled against Aristotle. After all they come to very little :—that he had small eyes, and thin legs, and a lisping utterance; that he passed a wild and spendthrift youth; that he was showy and affected in his attire, and habitually luxurious in his table; that he chose to live at the Macedonian court for the sake of the flesh-pots to be obtained by so doing; and that he was ungrateful to Plato,—these make up the sum of the charges against him. Perhaps if we knew all the facts, we might find that a contradictory, or at all events a different, statement would be more correct under each of the several heads. As it is, we may fairly deal with these imputations as we should with similar aspersions on the personal history of any great man, if they could neither be proved nor disproved, and set them aside as beneath consideration.

We cannot expect to know more than the outline of Aristotle's life, but all we know gives us the impression of a life that, morally speaking, was singularly honourable and blameless. And it was the life of one who by his intellectual achievements placed himself at the very head of ancient thought, and won the admiration and allegiance of many centuries. What those intellectual achievements were we have now to endeavour to set forth.

CHAPTER II.

THE WORKS OF ARISTOTLE.

A CATALOGUE of the works of Aristotle has been handed down to us, which was made by the librarian of the great Library at Alexandria about the year 220 B.C.—that is to say, a century after the death of the philosopher—and which gives the titles of all the books, contained in the Library, which were attributed to the authorship of Aristotle. These titles amount to 146 in number, but it is at first sight a most astonishing circumstance that they do not in the least answer to the writings which we now possess under the name of the "works of Aristotle." All the books mentioned in the Alexandrian catalogue are now lost; only a few fragments of them have been preserved in the shape of extracts and quotations from them made by other writers; but everything tends to show that they were quite a different set, and different altogether in character, from the forty treatises which stand collectively on our bookshelves labelled 'Aristotelis Opera.' Under the circumstances it would be natural to conjecture that so (comparatively speaking) short a time after the death of Aristotle, the learned keepers of the Alexandrian Library must have known what he really wrote, and therefore that in losing the books mentioned in the Alexandrian catalogue we have lost the true works of Aristotle, as they existed 100 years after his death, and that what has come down to us under his name, be it what it may, cannot be the genuine article. Other facts, however, and criticism of the whole question, show that this natural supposition is incorrect, and that something like the contradictory of it is true. It is a curious story, and needs some little explanation.

The life of Aristotle after his boyhood fell, as we have seen, into three broad divisions — namely, his first residence at Athens, from his eighteenth to his thirty-eighth year; his residence away from Athens, at Atarneus, Mitylene, Pella, and Stageira, from his thirty-eighth to his fiftieth year; and his second residence at Athens, from his fiftieth to his sixty-third year. During the first period, after studying under Plato, he commenced authorship by writing dialogues, which appear to have been published at the time. They differed from the Platonic dialogues in not being dramatic, but merely expository, like the dialogues of Bishop Berkeley, the principal *rôle* in each being assigned to Aristotle himself. They were somewhat rhetorical in style, and quite adapted for popular reading. In them Aristotle attacked Plato's doctrine of Ideas, and set forth views on philosophy, the chief good, the arts of government, moral virtue, and other topics. Then came the second period of his life, when he had definitely broken with the school of Plato, and was away from all the schools of Athens, enjoying much leisure and positions of dignity. In this period it is probable that he not only prosecuted his researches and independent speculations in many branches of thought and science, but that he learned to know his own mission in the world, which was to stick to the matter of knowledge, abandoning all regard for the artistic adornment of truth. During this period we may believe that he thoroughly developed the individual character of his own mind in relation to philosophy, so that when he came back to Athens he had quite established his own peculiar style of writing, crabbed indeed and inelegant, but full of an exact phraseology which he had himself constructed, and on the whole not unsuited as a vehicle for the exposition of science. We are not able, however, to say for certain whether in his second period he actually composed any works, though he must constantly have been compiling notes and memoranda, to serve either as the materials or the ground-plans for future treatises. The third period of Aristotle's life was the rich fruit-time of his genius. We have already mentioned how he set himself to the construction of an entire encyclopædia of science and philosophy. What we possess as his works contain the unfinished, but much advanced, working out of that project. There is every reason to believe that the great bulk of this series of writings was composed by Aristotle during the last thirteen years of his life. He was doubtless assisted by his school, and he must have had many treatises on hand at one time, or rather he had them all in his head, and when anything caused him to drop one for a time he could go on with another. Hardly any of the treatises are finished, still less is there any trace of careful revision and "the last hand." It is certain that many of these works were never published during Aristotle's lifetime, and it is even a question whether any of them were so published.

When Aristotle died, all the MSS of his later compositions, together with the considerable library of other men's writings which he had got together, were under charge of his chief disciple Theophrastus at the school in the Lyceum. After his decease, the Peripatetics appear to have worked to some extent at editing the uncompleted treatises, and at patching together those which existed as yet only in disjointed fragments. But there does not seem to have been any multiplication of copies, or what we should call "publication." On the death of Theophrastus (which took place thirty-five years later than that of Aristotle), the whole Peripatetic school-library went by his bequest to a favourite pupil named Neleus, who took all the rolls away with him to his home at a place called Scepsis, in the Troad. Included among them were the MSS, many of them unique, of Aristotle's most important works, which were thus removed from Europe. Not only was this the case, but a few years later the kings of Pergamus began seizing the books of private individuals in order to fill their own royal library, and the family of Neleus, afraid of losing the treasures they possessed,—which, however, they could little appreciate,—hid away the Peripatetic rolls and the precious MSS of Aristotle in a subterranean vault, where they remained for 150 years forgotten by the world. At the end of that interval, the dynasty of the kings of Pergamus having passed away, the books were brought out of their hiding-place and sold to one Apellicon, a wealthy Peripatetic and book-collector, who resided at Athens. They were said to have been by this time a good deal damaged by worms and damp; yet still it was a great thing that, after 187 years' absence, the best productions of Aristotle should be restored, about 100 B.C., to the West.

The termination of this "strange eventful history" was that in 86 B.C. Athens was taken by Sylla, and the library of Apellicon was seized and brought to Rome, where it was placed under the custody of a librarian, and several literary Greeks, resident in Rome, had access to it. Tyrannion, the learned friend of Cicero, got permission to arrange the MSS, and Andronicus of Rhodes, applying himself with earnestness to the task of obtaining a correct text and furnishing a complete edition of the philosophical works of Aristotle, arranged the different treatises and scattered fragments under their proper heads, and getting numerous transcripts made, gave publicity to a generally received text of Aristotle. There seems to be good reason for believing that "*Our* Aristotle," as Grote calls it, in contradistinction to the Aristotle of the Alexandrian Library,—is none other than this recension of Andronicus. And this being the case, we may well reflect how great was the risk which these works incurred of being consigned to perpetual oblivion. A few more years in the cellar at Scepsis, or any one of a hundred other accidents which might have prevented these writings from getting into the appreciative and competent hands of Tyrannion and Andronicus, would in all probability have made them as if they had never been. And thus that which was actually the chief intellectual food of men in the middle ages would have been withheld. Whether for better or worse, men's thoughts would have had a different exercise and taken a different direction. Much of ecclesiastical history would have been changed. And many of the modes in which we habitually think and speak at the present day would have been different from what they are.

But we must return to the Alexandrian catalogue. If the MSS of all Aristotle's most important works were carried off in the year 287 B.C., to be buried in Asia Minor for a century and a half, what means this list of 146 books bearing the name of Aristotle, which in 220 B.C. were stored up in the Alexandrian Library? Were these also all really written by Aristotle? Was he so voluminous a composer, as this would imply, as well as a profound thinker and an original explorer of nature in many departments? Or were the books supplied to the Alexandrian collection, as the works of Aristotle, mere forgeries, got up for the market, to supply the place of the genuine writings, which for the time had been lost to the world? The only answer that can be given to these questions must be a conjectural one, and probability seems to dictate an answer lying between the two extreme hypotheses. Several of the names appearing in the catalogue remind us of the titles of Plato's dialogues,—for instance 'Nerinthus,' 'Gryllus; or, On Rhetoric,' 'Sophist,' 'Menexenus,' 'Symposium,' 'The Lover,' 'Alexander; or, On Colonies,' &c. And the natural supposition is that these books, or some of them, were none other than these early dialogues which Aristotle composed during his first residence in Athens. Strabo says distinctly that when, by the bequest of Theophrastus, the Aristotelian MSS were taken away, the Peripatetic school had none of his works left except a few of the more popular ones. His dialogues had been published, and were available, and no doubt copies of them formed the nucleus of the books professing to be his in the Alexandrian Library. Others of the collection may have been excerpts from his greater works which had been made by his scholars, and were so kept before the world when the entire works themselves were hidden in Asia Minor. Many others were probably monographs and papers by members of the Peripatetic school, drawn up in Aristotle's manner, perhaps containing his ideas, and from a sort of reverential feeling attributed to him and inscribed with his name. The residue must have been forgeries pure and simple: imitations of his dialogues, and of such parts of his treatises as were known. All the books in the Alexandrian list, though they were numerous, appear to have been short, treating generally of isolated questions, and quite unlike the long methodical setting forth of entire sciences, such as we find in the writings of Aristotle that have came down to us.

The "fate of Aristotle's works" is a romantic episode

in the history of literature. But we must observe that what in the first place rendered this train of circumstances possible was the rapid decay of genius in Greece. When Aristotle died, none of his scholars was worthy to succeed him and carry on his work. His school do not seem to have appreciated what was great and valuable in his philosophy. They went off either into rhetorical sermonising on moral questions, or else into isolated inquiries, the solution of problems, or the drawing up of "papers" like those read before the Royal Society. It was perhaps a feeling of contempt for the Peripatetic school which induced Theophrastus, a generation after the death of Aristotle, to give away their whole library, including the great works of their master, to a foreign student. But for their apathy those great works would never have been left in unique copies, and ultimately exposed to such extreme peril. There must, however, have been a corresponding apathy in the external public, else curiosity would have demanded, and the love of science would have preserved, the results of Aristotle's later years. But the reading world of the third century B.C. seems to have been quite content to be put off with that which was really un-Aristotelian, though it bore the name of Aristotle—with immature, rhetorical dialogues, the work of his youth, or spurious imitations of that work, with excerpts, epitomes, "papers," and the sweepings of the Peripatetic school.

We may take Cicero, though living two centuries later, as a good specimen of the attitude towards Aristotle of a cultivated man of literature, not devoid of a certain taste for philosophy, of those times. Cicero often mentions, praises, and quotes Aristotle, but it is not, "*our* Aristotle," but the Aristotle of Alexandria, the writer of dialogues. Several passages of these dialogues have been translated and preserved by Cicero, who extols the "golden flow of their language," using terms which are as far as possible from being applicable to the harsh, compressed, and difficult style of Aristotle's scientific treatises. The latter were, indeed, too difficult and too repulsive for Cicero, as is plain from the story which he himself relates: Cicero had in his Tusculan villa some of the works of Aristotle, as we at present possess them, probably copies of the recension of Andronicus; when asked by his friend Trebatius what the 'Topics' of Aristotle were about, he advised him "for his own interest" to study the book for himself, or else to consult a certain learned rhetorician. Trebatius, however, was repelled by the obscurity of the writing, and the rhetorician, when consulted, confessed his total ignorance of Aristotle. Cicero thinks this no wonder, since even the philosophers know hardly anything about him, though they "ought to have been attracted by the incredible flow and sweetness of the diction." He then proceeds to give Trebatius a summary of the first few pages of the 'Topics' of Aristotle, which he had apparently read up for the occasion. From facts like this, it may be concluded that in the two last centuries before the Christian era, it was only the lighter and less valuable compositions of Aristotle that were generally known and admired. His more serious and really valuable contributions to thought and knowledge were left out of sight, ignored, and forgotten. For the moment it seemed as if the favourite dictum of Lord Bacon had come to pass—that "Time, like a river, bringing down to us things which are lighter and more inflated, lets what is more weighty and solid sink." But the result of that concatenation of accidents which we have narrated, was completely to reverse this sentence; so that now it may be said that all the lighter part of Aristotle's work has been swept away by the stream of Time, while only that which was weighty and solid has been suffered to remain in existence. Owing to the wealth of the Roman empire, it is likely that numerous copies were made of the entire works of Aristotle, as edited by Andronicus—both for public libraries and for individuals. This gave him a better chance of survival in a collective form during the wreck and destruction of the barbarian invasions; and afterwards he was early taken into the protection of the Church. The dialogues, in the meantime, and other shorter productions, which had figured in the Alexandrian catalogue, had no coherence with each other, and thus were not reproduced by the copyists and librarians, as a whole. Again, they did not attract, as the greater works of Aristotle did, the attention of successive scholiasts and commentators. In short, they fell into the neglect which, comparatively speaking, they deserved, and disappeared, all but a few scattered quotations. But now we can thank the Providence of history that we possess a large portion of the best of all that Aristotle thought and wrote. We possess it, indeed, incomplete as he left it, and not only so, but also edited and re-edited, transposed occasionally, interpolated, and eked out, by the earlier Peripatetics, by Andronicus, and perhaps by subsequent hands. Yet still the individuality of the Stagirite shines out through the greater part of these remains, and in studying them we feel that we are brought into contact with his mind.

If the supposition be correct that what we now possess is substantially the edition of Andronicus, it is clear in the first place that he did not mean this to be what we should call a "complete edition of the collective works of Aristotle," else he would have included in it the dialogues that Cicero quotes, the hymn in honour of Hermeias, and we know not what beside. His object appears to have been to give to the world the philosophy of Aristotle, hitherto virtually unknown, as he found it in the documents contained in the library of Apellicon. He dealt, it must be remembered, not only with that collection of rolls which had been buried in the Troad, but also with all the books which had been got together by a wealthy bibliophilist. The edition of Andronicus, if it corresponds with ours, contained a body of Aristotelian science and all Aristotle's greatest works; but on the one hand it excluded his less important writings, and on the other hand it admitted works which Aristotle certainly never wrote, though they are full of his ideas. Andronicus may have doubted as to the authorship of these treatises, which modern criticism pronounces to be by later Peripatetic hands;* or he may have thought that they

* One of the doubtful treatises—the 'Rhetoric dedicated to Alexander'—is supposed to be the work of Anaximenes, a writer contemporary with Aristotle.

represented or explained Aristotle, and might advantageously be preserved as part of his system. However it came about, we find included within the Aristotelian canon a treatise 'On the Universe,' neatly epitomising his views, but quite later than his time; one 'On the Motion of Animals' of which the same may be said; two treatises on morals, the 'Eudemian Ethics,' and the 'Great Ethics,' which are mere paraphrases of the 'Ethics' of Aristotle; a large book of 'Problems,' with their solutions, evidently of mixed authorship; a set of 'Opuscula,' or minor works, which belong to the class of Peripatetic monographs,—*e.g.* 'On Colours,' 'On Indivisible Lines,' 'On Strange Stories,' 'Physiognomics,' &c.; a treatise on 'Rhetoric,' quite different in principles from that of Aristotle's, and only suggested to be his by a fictitious dedication to Alexander, which has been stuck on to it. One or two other suspicious books might be mentioned, but even if everything were deducted against which the most sceptical criticism can make objection, less than one-fourth would be taken away from the entire mass which is in use to be labelled "Aristotle." The whole works in Bekker's octavo edition fill 3786 pages, and out of these the books, about whose genuineness any question has been raised, occupy only 925 pages. A solid residue remains, which may now be briefly characterised, merely in regard to its external form, a few remarks being added as to the chronological order in which it seems probable that Aristotle composed the various parts.

The remains of Aristotle come before us as a torso, —an incomplete and somewhat mutilated group from antiquity. Yet they constitute a whole, and the different treatises have an organic connection with each other. On the one hand, these works constitute an encyclopædia, for they contain a *résumé* and reconstruction of the sciences so far as was possible in the fourth century B.C. But on the other hand, they are more than an encyclopædia, because they are a philosophy, in which the universe is explained from the point of view and according to the system of one individual thinker. In them thought and knowledge are mapped out in broad and lucid outlines, with the details sometimes very fully worked in, sometimes barely indicated and left to be supplied by subsequent workers. The key to their arrangement is to be sought from Aristotle himself. From him we learn that science is divided into Practical, Constructive, and Theoretical. Practical science deals with man and human action, and this branch is copiously developed by Aristotle in his 'Ethics' and 'Politics.' Constructive science treats of art and the laws by which it is to be governed. Towards this branch Aristotle has made but a brief, though valuable, contribution, in his unfinished or mutilated treatise 'On Poetry.' Theoretical science has three great subdivisions, Physics, Mathematics, and Theology, otherwise called First Philosophy or Metaphysics. For the section of Mathematics nothing appears done in these remains. Aristotle speaks often of Mathematics as a great and interesting science, capable of affording high mental delight; but he seems to have regarded it as something tolerably finished and settled in his own time, and therefore less requiring his attention than other departments. Had his life been prolonged to the age attained by Plato or Alexander von Humboldt, he might possibly have undertaken the setting forth of the philosophy of Mathematics. Physics, on the other hand—that is to say, the Physical and Natural Sciences—occupy 1447 pages, or fully one half, of the writings which are undoubtedly Aristotle's. In his physical treatises one mind may be seen grappling, at first hand, with the provinces of almost all the different "Sections" of the British Association. Natural Philosophy, Astronomy, Physiology, and Natural History, are all marvellously founded in these treatises, by masterly analysis and classification of existing knowledge on the different subjects, and by the arrangement of facts, or supposed facts, under leading scientific ideas. Twelve books on Metaphysics occupy about one-tenth of the genuine remains of Aristotle. These books are obviously patched together out of the fragments of two or three unfinished treatises. How far this was done by the earlier Peripatetics, and how far by Andronicus, we cannot tell. But we here possess probably some of Aristotle's latest thoughts. And the name "Metaphysics," or "the things which follow after Physics," was given to these books when they were put together, after Aristotle's death, to indicate both chronological sequence in the order of composition, and also that the subject treated of lay beyond and above all physical inquiry.

In briefly grouping out the works of Aristotle, we have hitherto omitted to mention a class of writings, very important, and amounting to one-seventh of the whole mass, and yet which do not belong to either Practical, Constructive, or Theoretic science,—which are not part of Philosophy, but treat of the method of thought and the laws of reasoning, and which thus constitute the instrument or " organ " of Philosophy— that is to say, the logical writings, which were collectively named by the Peripatetic school "the Organon" or instrument. These books stand first in modern editions of Aristotle, and, speaking generally, they appear to have been written first of all his extant works.

The chronological sequence of composition among Aristotle's treatises is determined by critics, conjecturally and approximately, entirely on internal evidence. There are frequent references from one treatise to another, but these cannot always be relied on. Often they are mere interpolations, not having been made by the original writer, but stuck in by the meddlesomeness of some editor or copyist; in other cases they are genuine, and indicate truly the order of composition. Another piece of evidence, more strictly internal and more to be depended on, is the greater or less development of doctrine contained in the different works respectively. Aristotle in the earlier, and still more in the second period of his life, had doubtless made great preparation for the writing of all his great works. Still, as he successively took up each subject and concentrated his attention upon it, he did not fail to develop and push further his previous thought upon it. Thus, for instance, the 'Rhetoric' is full of ethical remarks and ethical doctrine, but when we come to read the 'Ethics' we find the same ethical questions repeated and treated with far greater depth and precision; and we may reasonably conclude that the 'Ethics' was the later-written treatise of the two.

Following out indications of this kind, we arrive at the conclusion that Aristotle first took in hand the science of method, and that, of all his extant works, the 'Topics' (or Logic of Probability), were first written, all but the eighth book; next the 'Analytics' (or Logic of Demonstration); next the eighth book of the 'Topics;' next Books I. and II. of the 'Rhetoric' (which has to do with the setting forth of truth); and then the 'Sophistical Refutations' (or treatise on Fallacies), which belongs to logic, yet still has a connection with the art of rhetoric. After thus far treating of the method of knowledge and expression, Aristotle appears to have gone on to treat of the matter of knowledge, and to have commenced with the practical sciences. First he wrote his 'Ethics,' though these were not quite finished, and afterwards his 'Politics,' and then he was led on to take up constructive science, and to write his small work 'On Poetry,' after which he reverted to his 'Rhetoric,' which was a cognate subject, and added a third book to that treatise. He now proceeded, though leaving much that was unfinished behind him, to the composition of his great series of physical treatises. The first of these to be written was probably the 'Physical Discourse,' which unfolded the general notions of natural philosophy, and gave an account of what Aristotle conceived under the terms "Nature," "Motion," "Time," "Space,"

"Causation," and the like. After these *prolegomena* to physics, he went on to treat of the universe in orderly sequence, beginning with the divinest part, the circumference of the whole, or outer heaven, which, according to his views, bounded the world, being composed of ether, a substance distinct from that of the four elements. This region was the sphere of the stars; and below it, in the Aristotelian system, was the planetary sphere, with the seven planets (the sun and moon being reckoned among the number) moving in it. Both stars and planets he seems to have regarded as conscious, happy beings, moving in fixed orbits, and inhabiting regions free from all change and chance; and these regions formed the subject of his treatise 'On the Heavens.' Next to this he is thought to have composed his work 'On Generation and Corruption,' in order to expound those principles of physical change (dependent on the hot, the cold, the wet, and the dry), which in the higher parts of the universe had no existence. This treatise formed the transition to the sublunary sphere, immediately round the earth, in which the meteors and comets moved, and which was characterised by incessant change, and by the passing of things into and out of existence, and which became the subject of his next treatise—the 'Meteorologics.' The last book of this work brings us down to the earth itself, and indeed beneath its surface, for it discusses, in a curious theory, the formation of rocks and metals.

From this point Aristotle would seem to have started afresh with his array of physiological treatises, the first written of which may very likely have been that 'On the Parts of Animals,' as containing general principles of anatomy and physiology. Next it seems probable that the work 'On the Soul' was produced, which was a physiological account of the vital principle as manifested in plants, animals, and men. A set of Appendices, as we should now call them, on various functions connected with life in general, such as sensation, memory, sleep, dreaming, longevity, death, &c., were added by Aristotle to his work 'On the Soul.' Afterwards, the ten books of 'Researches on Animals,' and the five books 'On the Generation of Animals,' together with a minor treatise 'On the Progression of Animals,' and with a collection of 'Problems,' which Aristotle probably kept by him, and added to from time to time, made up the series of his physical and physiological writings, so far as he lived to complete them. Treatises 'On the Physiology of Plants,' and 'On Health and Disease,' had been promised by him, but were never achieved. Simultaneously with some of the works now mentioned, but in idea last of his writings, and intended to be the crown of them all, the 'Metaphysics' were probably in course of composition when the death of Aristotle occurred.

It has been generally fancied that Aristotle was a very voluminous writer, and Diogenes Laertius, in transcribing the 'Alexandrian Catalogue,' remarks of him that "he wrote exceedingly many books." *We*, however, have no reason for joining in this opinion. His genuine works that have come down to us, fill altogether less than 3000 pages, and this amount in mere point of quantity is not anything unusual or surprising. Even if these works were composed, as we suppose them for the most part to have been, during the last thirteen years of his life, still, so far as quantity alone is concerned, that does not imply more than the exercise of a persistent industry. Many another man besides Aristotle has written as much as 200 pages a-year for thirteen years successively. Nor is it necessary to credit Aristotle with any great bulk of writings beyond what we possess. The writings of his early life, the dialogues, sketches, memoranda, and first efforts of his philosophic pen, which got to Alexandria, need not be highly estimated, even as to mass. They were probably eked out, as we have seen, by Peripatetic imitators, and were thus made to assume larger proportions. One important piece of Aristotle's labour has perished, namely, his 'Collection of the Constitutions of Greek Cities.' This would have been of the utmost interest as contributing to our knowledge of ancient history; but it was merely a compilation of facts, and probably would not have filled more than 400 or 500 pages. On the whole, it is not for voluminousness that Aristotle is to be wondered at. The marvel begins when we come to contemplate the solid and compressed contents of his writings, their vast and various scope, and the amount of original thought given through them to the world. It would have been enough for any one man's lasting reputation to have created the science of Logic, as Aristotle did; but in addition to this he wrote as a specialist, a discoverer, and an organiser, on at least a dozen other of the greatest subjects, and on each of them he was for many centuries accepted as the one authority. Such a position it is of course impossible for any modern to attain, but it was given to the powerful mind of Aristotle to attain it, owing to the peculiar circumstances of his epoch, and to the course of succeeding history.

CHAPTER III.

THE 'ORGANON' OF ARISTOTLE.

"Organon," or "the instrument," was, as we have said, the name given by Aristotle's ancient editors to his collective works on Logic. And from this of course Bacon took the title of 'Novum Organum,' or "the new instrument," for his own work, in which the principles and method of modern science were to be developed. We find the 'Organon' of Aristotle, as it stands in our editions, to consist of six treatises, respectively entitled 'Categories,' 'On Interpretation,' 'First Series of Analytics,' 'Second Series of Analytics,' 'Topics,' and 'Fallacies.' The two first of these are quite short, both together filling less than 60 pages, but they have been more read and commented on, especially in the middle ages, than all the rest of Aristotle put together. Thousands of scholars, who considered themselves staunch Aristotelians, and as such fought the battle of Nominalism against the Platonists, knew not a word of Aristotle beyond these two treatises. And yet, unfortunately, it is open to considerable doubt whether either of the two was actually written by Aristotle himself.

During the first periods of his life, Aristotle had

gradually forged the chief doctrines of his philosophy, and a peculiar set of terms in which they were embodied. When he came to write continuously, in his third period, he often assumed these doctrines and terms as already known, having doubtless given them considerable publicity in oral discourse, if not in essays and short treatises which have now been lost. And thus it frequently happens that we meet with terms and doctrines the meaning of which has to be gathered by implication, as it is never explicitly stated. This is the case with Aristotle's celebrated doctrine of "the Categories," to which he repeatedly refers, without ever telling us clearly what position in his system it is meant to hold. Perhaps the simplest account of this doctrine is to say that it sprang from an analysis and classification, made by Aristotle, of the things which men speak of. "Category," in Greek, meant "speaking of" something. Now, when we speak of anything, we shall find (so Aristotle implies) that we are either speaking of "a substance,"—as, for instance, of a particular man; or else that we are asserting something to be the case about something else. And what we can assert about anything else must be either (1) some "quality" it possesses; (2) its "quantity;" (3) some "relation" in which it stands; (4) the "place" of its existence; (5) the "time" of its existence; (6) its "action," or what it does; (7) its "passion," or what is done to it; (8) its "attitude;" or (9) its "habit" or dress. "Substance," and the above nine modes of speaking of it make up the list of the Ten Categories, as enumerated by Aristotle in his 'Topics' (I. 9), and also in the little treatise which professes to treat especially of this subject.

A complete classification of the things which we can speak of must include everything that we can think of, and therefore all the world. But the "Ten Categories" of Aristotle cannot fail to strike us as a curious summary of all things in heaven and earth. Attitude and Habit, or Dress, the 9th and 10th "Categories," are so exclusively human that we are surprised to find them introduced among genera of far wider application. Some critics say that the list is both redundant in one way and deficient in another. They say that it is redundant because the whole thing might be cut down to two heads—Substance and Relation ; and deficient because to none of the " Categories" could mental states and feelings be appropriately assigned. However, Aristotle might perhaps have said that they came under Quality, Action, or Passion, as the case might be. In other parts of his works he gives enumerations of the "Categories," naming 8, 6, or 4, instead of 10. In one place ('Met.' VI. iv.) he names the first five "Categories," with "Motion" added as a sixth. This last would certainly, according to his view, include the various operations of the mind. On the whole, Aristotle does not appear to have laid much stress on his table of "Categories" as containing an exhaustive division of all things. Probably at first this table was the result of a study in language, made at a time when logical and even grammatical distinctions were in their infancy. Aristotle took the idea of a particular man—say Callias —and called this "Substance," and then tried how many different kinds of assertions could be made about him; and when he had reduced these to 9, he was perhaps pleased, because "Substance," and the 9 kinds of assertion made about it, made up 10 " Categories," and 10 is a perfect number. He afterwards dropped this particular number, and the " Categories " which had been brought in at the end of the list to eke it out. He seems always to have thought a classification of the ways in which we speak of things to be useful for obtaining clear notions. But he was far too sensible to apply his original table of " Ten Categories" as a Procrustean bed for measuring everything in the universe. At the same time it must be confessed that it has been prevalently thought that he did so. Thus Bacon contemptuously accused him of " constructing the world out of his 'Categories.'" But this arose very much from the fact that the first book of the 'Organon' was read out of all proportion more than Aristotle's great philosophical treatises, and so it came about that the Aristotelian schoolmen attached an exaggerated importance to the table of which it treats, and their sins have been imputed to the Stagirite himself.

The little book before us, which has exercised so much influence, might be described as a logical monograph on the characteristics of some of the "Categories." After naming the ten, without any account of the manner in which they are arrived at, it discusses to a certain extent the first four only. Then some chapters are appended, which may or may not have been originally a separate paper, on the different ways in which things are called "opposite," &c. There are two or three hypotheses possible about the book entitled 'Categories.' Either it was an early essay written by Aristotle himself, and preserved among his MSS; or it consists of notes from his school, made by some scholar during his lifetime; or else it is the work of some Peripatetic, drawn up after his death, when the making of such tracts had become a fashion. Style is not a sufficient guide in such a question, because the Peripatetics closely imitated the manner of their master. The chief reason for thinking that this book cannot have been his is on account of the extreme nominalism of its doctrine. Aristotle in the 'Metaphysics' (VI. vii. 4) asserts that the universal is the "first substance," while the individual has a secondary and derivative existence; but it is asserted in the 'Categories' that the individual is the first substance, and that if individuals were swept away universals would cease to exist. Aristotle may have said this in the early days of his antagonism against Plato;—if so, he seems to have reverted in maturer life to something nearer approaching, though distinguishable from, Plato's view. There are, however, unphilosophical and un-Aristotelian things in the book—as, for instance, the saying ('Cat.' vii. 21) that "if knowledge ceased to exist, the thing known might still remain." All this looks like the work of a clever but somewhat materialistic follower of the Peripatetic school.

The book which we find standing second in the 'Organon,' is the little treatise 'On Interpretation,' or, as it might be called, 'On Language as the interpreter of Thought.' Its subject is that which in Logic is called the "proposition,"—that is to say, it treats of sentences which affirm or deny something. Modern Logic is divided into three parts, treating respectively of terms, propositions, and syllogisms; and it might for a moment be supposed that the three works, 'Categories,' 'On Interpretation,' and 'Analytics,' correspond to these three divisions. But this is only superficially the case; for the 'Categories' does not treat generally of simple terms, it only touches on some characteristics of the names of Substances, Qualities, Quantities, and Relations. And the book, 'On Interpretation' is not a prelude to the 'Analytics;' it is a separate logical monograph on some of the characteristics of propositions, containing, at the same time, some remarks on words, as fit or unfit to become terms—on indefinite words, "syn-categorematic" words, &c. The great merit of this little treatise is undeniable, especially when considered as containing matter, which though now long accepted and perfectly trite, was in a great measure new in the time of Aristotle, and which served towards the clearing up of many a confusion. All those clear statements about the nature of the proposition; on what is meant by "contrariety" and "contradiction;" on "modal propositions," or propositions in which the amount of certainty is expressed by the words "necessarily" or "probably;" and other points which the reader will find in the second part of Whately's 'Logic,' are taken almost *verbatim* from this treatise. There is one point of which Whately was especially fond—namely, that "truth" is the attribute of a proposition or assertion and of nothing else, except in a metaphorical way. This comes from the work before us, where it is laid down as the first characteristic of a proposition that it must be either true or false. A distinction, however, is here drawn, for propositions admit the idea of time. Now, it is the case with regard to propositions of past and present time—for instance, "it is raining," or "it rained yesterday"—that they must either be true or false; but with regard to future propositions this is not the case; for suppose we say "there will be a battle to-morrow between the Turks and Servians"—this may be probable or improbable, but it is neither true nor false. Obviously, there is no existing fact with which to compare such propositions, and thus to pronounce on their truth or falsehood. But it is argued here that if future propositions, or prophecies, could be pronounced to be certainly true, it would do away with human agency and freewill. This may seem hardly worth enunciating, but it was new at the time when this book was written.

The writer, in considering "modal propositions," which assert things as necessary, probable, or possible, introduces some discussion on "possibility," and mentions three heads of the possible. Ordinarily, things in this world are first possible, and then become realised, or actual; but there is another class of things which are always actual, and the possibility in them is only latent or implied—such are the "first substances" which have existed from all eternity; and thirdly, there is a class of things which always seem possible, and yet can never be realised—for instance, the greatest number or the least quantity, which, while we speak of them, no one can ever say that he has reached. In this passage we find ourselves rather in the region of Metaphysics than of Logic, and it is remarkable that here the phrase "first substances" is used, not, as in the 'Categories,' to denote ordinary individual existences on the earth, but as a term to denote the eternal, primeval substances which have never not been, such as, in Aristotle's view, were the stars, and sun, and planets.

The treatise 'On Interpretation' was evidently not written at the same time with the 'Categories,' or is by a different author, and on a different plane of thought. It is more philosophical and more Aristotelian; it quotes both the 'Analytics' and the work 'On the Soul,' and therefore cannot be an early production of the Stagirite's. There is a tradition that Andronicus of Rhodes held that this treatise was not written by Aristotle at all, while Ammonius, a great commentator, argued in favour of its genuineness. Their arguments, which have been preserved, do not seem conclusive one way or the other. Perhaps the only reason against considering this to have been the writing of Aristotle himself is, that while it obviously is as late as the period of his great treatises, it is not in the manner of those treatises. On the whole, it seems safest to conclude that this little book must consist of the notes of Aristotle's oral teaching upon the elementary bases of Logic, faithfully recording his ideas, and often the very words which he had used.

We may set aside, then, the 'Categories' and the 'Interpretation' as of doubtful origin, and as at all events not having been originally intended for the place which they have so long held in the forefront of the writings of Aristotle. We turn to that which was, so far as we know, in reality the opening treatise of the Aristotelian Encyclopædia—namely, the 'Topics;' and there is some peculiarity to be remarked in the very fact that the subject with which it deals should have been the first to be taken in hand. We know that Aristotle founded, and all but completed, the science of Logic; but we are apt to forget that, when he began to write, the very idea that there was, or could be, such a science had never come into anybody's head. What philosophers then knew about, and practised, and formulated, was not Logic, or the science of the laws of reasoning, but Dialectic, or the art of discussion. This art was by no means confined to philosophers, but it was the fashion of the day, and was widely and constantly in use in Athenian society, as an intellectual game or fencing-match. The dialogues of Plato give us dramatic specimens of the encounter of wits which might be seen exhibited in numerous Athenian circles from the middle of the fifth century B.C. down to the time of Aristotle. That restless and intellectual people who, three and a half centuries later, were described as "spending their time in nothing else but either to tell or to hear some new thing," were at an earlier period possessed by an insatiate appetite for discussion and controversy, whether with a view to truth or to mere victory over an opponent. Dialectic then, as an art, was thoroughly recognised, and all but universally practised, yet still the fundamental principles on which it must rest had never yet been properly drawn out, and Aristotle seems to have felt it to be the first task for one who would build up the entire fabric of knowledge, to lay down the laws of Dialectic as the art and science of method. "Dialectic," he says, "is useful for three things: for exercise of the mind, for converse with other men, and for knowing how to question and handle the principles of philosophy." And the object of his 'Topics' is, as he tells us, "to discover a method by which we shall be able to reason from probabilities on any given question, and to defend a position without being driven to contradict our own assertions."

Properly speaking, Dialectic, as defined by Aristotle, ought not to come first in the order of sciences, for it is a kind of applied reasoning; it is reasoning applied to that which is not certain, but only probable. Therefore the general principles of reasoning should be drawn out first, and then these should be shown in application to the certainties of science, after which a subordinate branch might be added on reasoning upon probabilities. Aristotle, however, as we have said, did not set out with the conception of Logic, or the science of reasoning, as existing by itself. This only gradually dawned upon him, and it was out of his researches in Dialectic that he was led to develop the idea of Logic. It was in thinking out the rules of Dialectic that Aristotle discovered the principles of the Syllogism, and he was justly proud of the discovery. There are only two passages in all his extant writings in which he speaks of himself: one is that in which he apologises for differing from Plato, "because truth must be preferred to one's friend;" the other is the passage at the end of the 'Fallacies' (which is a sort of appendix to the 'Topics'), where he refers to his services to Dialectic. "In regard to the process of syllogising," he says, "I found positively nothing said before me: I had to work it out for myself by long and laborious research." The discovery of the structure of the syllogism—that is to say, of the forms in which men do, and must, reason about a great many things in life, was of course very useful for dialectical purposes, both for exposing fallacy in others and for keeping one's self straight in controversy. But Aristotle, while in the course of writing his treatise on Dialectic, seems to have been impressed with the independent importance of the theory of the Syllogism, and of the necessity for a simple, unapplied Logic. So, after completing seven books of his 'Topics,' he dropped the subject, and went on to write his first and second series of 'Analytics;' and it was only after he had finished these two great works that he returned to complete the 'Topics,' by the addition of an eighth book.

The 'Topics,' as their name implies, are the books "treating of places," and "places" are seats of arguments, or matters in which arguments may be found. Aristotle in a long course of observation and analysis had apparently noted down the heads of reasonings most likely to be available for either attack or defence in dialectical controversy, and he here sets these forth in seven books. His object is to educate the reader to be a skilful dialectician in Athenian arenas. He names the four chief instruments for this purpose: 1st, To make a large collection of propositions—*i.e.*, authoritative sayings, whether of great men or of the many; 2d, To study the different senses in which terms are used; 3d, To detect differences; 4th, To note resemblances. The last three out of these four suggestions are expanded at great length, and Aristotle tells us how to use various logical distinctions, here brought forward for the first time, in pulling to pieces the arguments of an opponent—for instance, how to use the heads of predicables (*genus*, *differentia*, *proprium*, and *accidens*), or the categories, or the several kinds of logical opposition, for this purpose. The first seven books of the 'Topics' scarcely touch at all upon dialectical method, they are quite taken up with a wearisome and seemingly endless list of heads of argumentation. The eighth book, written later, adds some counsel upon the arrangement and marshalling of your arguments, whether you be the respondent defending a thesis, or the interrogator who attacks it. Some of these pieces of advice might be characterised as "dodges;" for instance, when we are told how to conceal from our adversary what we want to prove, till we have got him to admit something which would really imply the point we are aiming at. In Dialectic, as in love and war, almost everything was fair. And yet Aristotle concludes his treatise by saying, "You must, however, take care not to carry on this exercise with every one, especially with a vulgar-minded man. With some persons the dispute cannot fail to take a discreditable turn. When the respondent tries to make a show of escaping by unworthy manœuvres, the questioner on his part must be unscrupulous also in syllogising; but this is a disgraceful scene. To keep clear of such abusive discourse, you must be cautious not to discourse with commonplace, unprepared respondents."

Athenian Dialectic has passed away, though it had a faint and clumsy revival in the "Disputations" of the middle ages. Even as a preparation for ordinary controversy and debate, it is questionable whether a study of Aristotle's 'Topics' would nowadays be found useful, except so far as the logical distinctions which it contains might sharpen the intellect. But this latter result might equally well be attained by studying the ordinary logics into which all those distinctions have been transplanted. The 'Topics,' at the time when it was written, was a work of original penetration, and of vast accumulative labour. Aristotle perhaps ought to have foreseen that it would not be worth his while to reduce Athenian Dialectic to a methodised system, but he did not; and much of what he accumulated for one purpose, came to have great value for another. The chief merit of the 'Topics' of Aristotle is, that while intended to be the permanent regulator of Dialectic, it became in reality the cradle of Logic.

Aristotle himself did not use the word "Logic," which was probably invented afterwards by the Stoics; he spoke of "Analytic," by which he meant the science of analysing the forms of reasoning. We come now to his 'Prior and Posterior' (or First and Second Series of) 'Analytics.' In these works he has produced nothing temporary, or of merely antiquarian interest, but an addition to human knowledge as complete in itself, as permanent, and as irrefragable, as the Geometry of Euclid. It is true that Aristotle did not cover and exhaust the entire field in reasoning, just as Euclid did not exhaust the theory of all the properties of space. But so far as he went Aristotle was perfect. His work took its origin out of the examination of dialectical controversies, which, at the time when he wrote, much predominated over all that we should think worthy of the name of physical science, and therefore his aim was limited to the analysis of deductive reasonings. But men still reason deductively, and will always do so; during a great part of life we are employed, not in finding out new laws of nature, but in applying what we knew before, in appealing to general beliefs, or supposed classes of facts, and in drawing our positive or negative conclusions accordingly. To all this process, whenever it occurs, the 'Analytics' of Aristotle are as applicable as the principles of Geometry are to every fresh mensuration.

Aristotle invented the word "Syllogism," for the process of putting two assertions together and out of them deducing a third. This word indeed existed before in Greek literature, but in a general sense, meaning "computation," "reckoning" or "consideration." But Aristotle stamped it with the technical meaning which it has ever since borne. In introducing the word, however, it must not be supposed that he introduced, or invented, the process of reasoning to which he applied it, or that he ever pretended to do so. Yet he has been ridiculed, as if this had been the case—as for instance by Locke, who says that it would be strange if God had made men two-legged, and left it to Aristotle to make them rational! The grammarian who first distinguished nouns from verbs and gave them their names, did not invent nouns and verbs, but only called attention to their existence in language; and he who first made rules of syntax was only recording the ways in which men naturally speak and write, not making innovations in language; and so Aristotle with his "Syllogism" only clearly pointed out a process which had always, though unconsciously, been carried on. There is no doubt that, ever since they have possessed reason at all, men have made syllogisms, though, like M. Jourdain making prose, they have for the most part been unaware of it.

The 'First Series of Analytics' is entirely devoted to the theory of the Syllogism, with a few collateral discussions. It has no connection with the treatise 'On Interpretation,' from which, in phraseology and some points of doctrine, it differs. It is a work which must excite our wonder if we consider the serried mass of observations which it contains, and the absolutely complete way in which it constructs a science and provides for it an appropriate nomenclature. Though countless generations of commentators and school-men have been busy with the 'Analytics,' and many modern philosophers have independently treated of Logic, none of them have been able to add a single point of any importance to Aristotle's theory of deductive reasoning. The 'Analytics' are of course not light reading. The style is severely scientific, and concisely expository; not a single grace of ornament, not a superfluous word, is admitted. As Aristotle introduced into these treatises a copious use of the letters A, B, C, to denote the three terms of the syllogism, many parts read like Euclid with the diagrams omitted. It is not necessary to attempt any further description of the contents, or to give here an account of the figures and moods of syllogisms, of conversion of propositions, reduction of syllogisms to the first figure, and the rest, because all these things have found their way into modern compendiums. Are they not written in Aldrich, and Mansel, and Whately, and many other books?

Yet there is one passage of the 'Prior Analytics' which we must quote in bare justice to Aristotle. Owing to the too exclusive study of his logical works in the middle ages, and owing to modern writers identifying him with the absurdities of his followers, an idea arose that he, like the least judicious of the schoolmen, thought that all reasoning should be through syllogisms, that nature could be expounded by means of syllogisms, and that syllogisms were a source of knowledge. Hence came protests like that of Bacon, that "the syllogism is unequal to the subtlety of nature." But nothing could be further from the truth than the whole idea. The reader may be assured that on a point of this kind Aristotle was as sensible as Lord Bacon or John Stuart Mill. After showing that syllogisms are constantly used, and after analysing their form, and showing on what their validity depends, he proceeds to make some remarks on the way in which the major premiss, or general statement in the syllogism, is to be obtained. He says ('Prior Anal.' I. xxx.): "There is the same course to be pursued in philosophy, and in every science or branch of knowledge. *You must study facts.* Experience alone can give you general principles on any subject. This is the case in astronomy, which is based on the observation of astronomical phenomena; and it is the case with every branch of science or art. When the facts in each branch are brought together, it will be the province of the logician to set out the demonstrations in a manner clear and fit for use. When the investigation into nature is complete, you will be able in some cases to exhibit a demonstration; in other cases you will have to say that demonstration is not attainable." Bacon knew very little Aristotle at first hand; and he cannot have known this passage, else its overwhelming good sense must have stopped many of his remarks. And Aristotle in practice was quite true to the principles here announced. In his 'Ethics,' 'Politics,' and 'Physics,' he does not pedantically drag in the syllogism, but masses facts together, and makes penetrating remarks upon them, and discusses freely, by means of analogy, comparison, and intuition, very much as the ablest writers of the present day would do.

At the same time it must be admitted that, after fully explaining the deductive process, he left the theory of the inductive process, by which general laws are ascertained, almost entirely unexplored. He briefly observes ('Prior Anal.' II. xxiii.) that "induction, or the syllogism that arises from it, consists in proving the major term of the middle by means of the minor." In other words, suppose that we are proving that animals without a gall are long-lived, we do so through our knowledge that man, the horse, and the mule have no gall. Now, in a natural deductive syllogism, we should say—

>All animals without a gall are long-lived;
>Man, the horse, and the mule, have no gall;
>Therefore they are long-lived.

"Long-lived" is here the major term; but in the inductive process we prove it of the middle term, "animals without a gall," by means of the minor term, "man, the horse, and the mule." So we require to state the inductive syllogism thus:—

Man, the horse, and the mule are long-lived;
Man, the horse, and the mule are animals without a gall;
Therefore (all) animals without a gall are long-lived.

Aristotle adds that, for the validity of this reasoning, you require to have an intuition in your reason that "man, the horse, and the mule" are, or adequately represent, the whole class of animals without a gall. This is, in fact, the crucial question in the inductive process—Do the instances you have got adequately represent the whole class of similar instances, so as to give you the key to a law of nature? For instance, if it is found that in two or three cases a particular treatment cures the cholera, how can you tell whether the induction is adequate, and that you are justified in asserting, as a general principle, that "such and such a treatment cures the cholera"? Modern logic tells us that a statement of the kind requires verification; and modern writers, such as Bacon, Whewell, and Mill, are at great pains to point out the best methods of verification,—which after all consist in observing and experimenting further; in eliminating all accidental circumstances; in recording, and, if possible, accounting for, the facts which go against your principle; and, finally, in either rejecting it as unproven, or bringing it out as completely established after passing through the ordeal of thorough examination. But the minute and cautious methods of experiment and observation which have gradually come into use among scientific men in modern times were unknown in the days of Aristotle; so it is not to be wondered at that, having so much else to think of, he did not enter upon this field of inquiry. He tells us repeatedly that we must draw our general principles from familiarity with particular facts; but instead of suggesting methods of verification for the validity of those principles, he merely says that they must have the sanction of our reason. It seems to have been his idea that, after gathering facts up to a certain point, a flash of intuition would supervene, telling us, "This is a law." Such, no doubt, has often been the case, as in Newton's famous discovery of the law of gravitation from seeing an apple fall. Yet still, in the ordinary course of science, verification ought always to be at hand. And Aristotle, in omitting to provide for this, left a blank in his theory of the acquirement of knowledge.

Aristotle, like Plato, drew a strong line of demarcation between matters in which you can have, and those in which you cannot have, certainty; in other words, between the region of opinion and the region of science. Syllogistic reasoning is applicable both to certainties and probabilities, and as such it had been formally drawn out in the 'First Analytics.' Its application by means of Dialectic to matters of opinion had been set forth (in anticipation of the natural order of treatment) in the 'Topics;' and now Aristotle proceeded in his 'Second Series of Analytics' to write the logic of science, and to exhibit the syllogism as the organ of demonstration.

The attitude of Science is of course different from that of Dialectic. In Dialectic two disputants are required, one of whom is to maintain a thesis, while the other by questioning is to endeavour to draw from him some admission which shall be repugnant to that thesis. In Science, on the other hand, we are not to suppose two disputants, but a teacher and a learner. Thus the 'Second Analytics' begin with the words— "All teaching and all intellectual learning arises out of previously existing knowledge." This points at once to a characteristic of Aristotle's view of Science. In modern times we associate Science most commonly with the idea of the inductive accumulation of knowledge; and thus we talk of "scientific inquiry;" but Aristotle thinks of Science as deductive and expository, and identifies it with "teaching." If we look at the specimens of scientific reasoning which he gives us in this book, we shall find that a large proportion of them are taken from Geometry. Next to this, the science most frequently appealed to is Astronomy. But he also mentions Arithmetic, Optics, Mechanics, Stereometry, Harmonics, and Medicine. Sometimes he refers to questions of Natural History, and at other times to questions of Botany. He even applies his scientific method to Ethics, and shows how we are to obtain a definition of the virtue of magnanimity, by observing the leading characteristics of those who are called magnanimous. The Sciences are not classified here, but a comparative scale of perfection among them is indicated; and those are generally laid down to be the most perfect Sciences which are the most elementary and abstract. But with all this leaning towards an ideal of pure and abstract science, it is remarkable how much the Sciences of Observation are considered in this book, and what an enlightened and modern atmosphere breathes through many parts of it.

In developing his idea of Science, Aristotle takes occasion to controvert several opinions which had found vogue in his day. One of these was that everything in Science could be proved. Some men had a notion that you could go back *ad infinitum* in proving the principles from which your science was deduced: "This principle was true because of that, and that because of something else, and so on for ever." Others fancied that by a kind of circular reasoning the propositions of Science might all be made to prove each other. "No," says Aristotle, "Science must commence from something that is not proved at all." Science must start from *im-mediate* principles—*i.e.*, principles that cannot be established by any middle term, or, in other words, by any syllogistic reasoning. The axioms of Euclid may give us a specimen of such principles, but, according to Aristotle, each science had its own "primary universal, and immediate principles;" these principles, we are distinctly told, are not innate, but the source of them is the Nous or Reason, which (as we have seen) attains them intuitively, when sufficiently advised, so to speak, by a course of inductive observation. Again, Aristotle brings out here his opposition to Plato's theory of Ideas: he says, that it is not necessary for Science that the Ideas of things should have a separate existence, but only that universal ideas, or genera, should be capable of being predicated of many individuals. This view seems to correspond with what, in modern times, has been called Conceptualism, and which is a compromise between Nominalism and Realism.

These, however, are metaphysical distinctions. Another point more closely belonging to the Logic of Science is brought out against Plato—namely, the separateness of the Sciences, which follows from each Science having its own appropriate principles. Plato conceived, or appeared to do so, that from the principles of Philosophy (*i.e.*, Metaphysics), right doctrines of Ethics and Politics could be deduced. Hence he said, "It will never be well with the State till the kings are philosophers, or the philosophers kings." Aristotle, on the other hand, considered the speculative conception of the good, as entertained by a metaphysician, to be quite distinct from the practical conception of the good which occupies the statesman or the moralist. In many ways this demarcation by Aristotle of the separate spheres of different Sciences, gave rise to great clearness of view.

The Logic of Science deals, as might be expected, with the method of defining things,—that is, of saying what they are. But we do not here find the scholastic idea of definition, *per genus et differentiam*, by stating the class to which a thing belongs, and the characteristic which separates it from the rest of that class. Aristotle takes the more real and thorough position that, to define a thing adequately, you must state its cause. "Science itself," he says, "is knowledge of a cause." But what is cause? There are four kinds: the "formal," which is the whole nature of a thing, being the sum of the other three causes; the "material," or the antecedents out of which the thing arises; the "efficient," or motive power; and the "final," or object aimed at. Speaking generally, the causes most in use for scientific definitions are the efficient and the final. We define an eclipse of the moon by its efficient cause,—the interposition of the earth. We define a house by its final cause,—a structure for the sake of shelter.

One quotation, as a specimen, may conclude these glimpses of the 'Later Analytics,' or Aristotle's Logic of Science: "Nature," he says, "presents a perpetual cycle of occurrences. When the earth is wet with rain, an exhalation rises; when an exhalation rises, a cloud forms; when a cloud forms, rain follows, and the earth is saturated: so that the same term recurs after a cycle of transformations. Every occurrence has another for its consequent, and this consequent another, and so on, till we are brought round to the primary occurrence."

After finishing his 'Later Analytics,' Aristotle seems to have taken up Rhetoric, and to have written the main part of his treatise on that subject. He then reverted to Dialectic, and completed his exposition of it by writing his book on 'Sophistical Confutations,' which now stands as the conclusion of the 'Organon.' The matter treated of in this book has a close connection with that treated of in the 'Topics.' The practice of Dialectic at Athens had given scope to a class, which gradually arose, of professional and paid disputants, or professors and teachers of the art of controversy. This professional class, who were called the "Sophists," got a bad name in antiquity; and Aristotle treats them disparagingly as mere charlatans. Thus while Contentiousness is arguing for victory, he describes Sophistry as arguing for gain. The Sophist, according to Aristotle, tried to confute people and make them look foolish, employing for this purpose, not fair arguments, but quibbles and fallacies; and all this was done in order to be thought clever and to get pupils. An amusing picture of this sort of process is given in Plato's dialogue called 'Euthydemus,' where two professionals are represented as bamboozling with verbal tricks an ingenuous youth, until Socrates by his dialectical acumen and superior wit rescues the victim from his tormentors, and turns the tables upon them. The following is a specimen of the "sophistical confutations" in 'Euthydemus:' "Who learn, the wise or the unwise?" "The wise," is the reply; given with blushing and hesitation. "And yet when you learned you did not know and were not wise." "Who are they who learn the dictation of the grammar-master, the wise boys or the foolish boys?" "The wise." "Then after all the wise learn." "And do they learn what they know or what they do not know?" "The latter." "And dictation is a dictation of letters?" "Yes." "And you know letters?" "Yes." "Then you learn what you know." "But is not learning acquiring knowledge?" "Yes." "And you acquire that which you have not got already?" "Yes." "Then you learn that which you did not know." *

Plato's picture is, doubtless, a caricature, exaggerating the fallacious practice of the lower sort of professional disputants to be met with in those days at Athens. But the dialogue 'Euthydemus' seems to have suggested to the scientific mind of Aristotle the idea of classifying all the fallacies that had been or could be employed in argument, and the 'Sophistical Confutations' is the result. To the value of this book it makes no difference how far the quibbles and deceptive reasonings adduced had been actually used by certain definite individuals for mercenary purposes, or whether, historically speaking, the professional "Sophists" of Greece were as bad as Plato had represented them. Putting the "Sophists" of Greece quite out of consideration, fallacy, whether voluntary or involuntary,

* See Professor Jowett's Introduction to 'Euthydemus' in his 'Dialogues of Plato,' i. p. 184, 2d ed.

will still remain, and is still always incident to human reasoning. And this it is which Aristotle undertakes to classify. It might be thought that errors in reasoning were infinite in number, and incapable of being reduced to definite species; but this is not the case, because every unsound reasoning is the counterfeit of some sound reasoning, and only gains credence as such. But the forms of sound reasoning are strictly limited in number, and therefore the forms of fallacy must be limited also. Ambiguity in language is, of course, one main source of fallacy; and fallacy arises whenever either the major, the minor, or the middle term of a syllogism is used with a double meaning. It will be seen above that the quibblers in 'Euthydemus' employ the terms "wise," "learn," and "know" in double senses so as to cause confusion.

Aristotle's account of the fallacies attaching to syllogistic or deductive reasoning is complete and exhaustive, and has been the source of all that has subsequently been written on the subject. The fallacies of *amphibolia, accidens, a dicto secundum quid ad dictum simpliciter, ignoratio elenchi, petitio principii, consequens, non causa pro causa,* and *plures interrogationes* have become the property of modern times, with names Latinised from those by which Aristotle first distinguished them; and in Whately's, and other compendiums, they may be found duly explained. It is true that Aristotle does not investigate the sources of error attaching to the inductive process; the "idols of the tribe" and "of the den" he left for Bacon to denounce; and the fallacies of "inspection," "colligation," and the rest to be supplied by Whewell and Mill. But with regard to this, it must be observed that he treats of the doctrine of Fallacies as supplementary, not to the Logic of Science, but to Dialectic. All through the 'Sophistical Confutations' we have a background of Hellenic disputation,—the questioner and the answerer are hotly engaged, and the bystanders keenly interested, — Aristotle in analysing fallacy is primarily contributing artistic rules for the conduct of the game. The local and temporary object has passed away, and much of the original importance of the book has accordingly been lost; but the distinctions which were here for the first time drawn out have passed over into Logic, and have doubtless contributed somewhat to clear up the thought and language of Europe.

CHAPTER IV.

ARISTOTLE'S 'RHETORIC' AND 'ART OF POETRY.'

WE have seen how Aristotle, when a young man, during his first residence at Athens, opened a school of Rhetoric, in rivalry to the veteran Isocrates. During his second residence, he presided over a school, not of Rhetoric alone, but of Philosophy and of all knowledge. Yet it is said that in the Peripatetic school "Rhetoric was both scientifically and assiduously taught." * Rhetoric had now, however, become for Aristotle merely one in that wide range of sciences, each of which he had set himself, as far as possible, to bring to perfection. He turned to it, in due course, from his achievements in Logic, and produced his great treatise on this subject. Goethe said of his 'Faust' that "he had carried it for twenty years in his head, till it had become pure gold." The first part of the 'Rhetoric' of Aristotle bears marks of having gone through a similar process. The outlines of its arrangement are characterised by luminous simplicity, the result of long analytic reflection; the scientific exposition is made

* Professor Jebb's 'Attic Orators,' ii. 431. See Diog. Laert., V. i. 3.

in a style which is, for Aristotle, remarkably easy and flowing; and each part of the subject is adorned with a wealth of illustration which indicates the accumulation of a lifetime.

Several treatises on Rhetoric had appeared in Greece before Aristotle sat down to write about it. Only one of these, but perhaps the best of them, has come down to us. Curiously enough it has been preserved among the works of Aristotle, as if it had been written by him, and it goes by the name of the 'Rhetoric addressed to Alexander,' having a spurious dedication to Alexander the Great tacked on to it. It is believed by scholars to be the work of Anaximenes of Lampsacus, an eminent historian and rhetorician contemporary with Aristotle. It is entirely practical in its aim, but it bears traces of the sophistical leaven, and deals overmuch in those tricks of argument and disputation which got the Sophists their bad name. The other lost systems of Rhetoric by Corax, Tisias, Antiphon, Gorgias, Thrasymachus, and others, appear to have been all strictly practical. Aristotle complains* that they confined themselves too much to treating of forensic oratory, and to expounding the methods best adapted for working on the feelings of a jury. His own aim is broader and more philosophical: while he defines Rhetoric as "the art of seeing what elements of per-

---

* There was another System of Rhetoric, which, perhaps, should not be included in this number—namely, the 'Rhetoric of Theodectes,' which Aristotle refers to in his third book (III. ix. 10), as containing a classification of prose periods. There was a tradition that Aristotle contributed an introduction to the 'Rhetoric of Theodectes.'

suasion attach to any subject," he traces out these "elements of persuasion" to their root in the principles of human nature.

The "sources of persuasion" Aristotle reduces to three heads: *first*, the personal character which the orator is able to exhibit or assume; *second*, the mood into which he is able to bring his hearers; *third*, the arguments or apparent arguments which he can adduce. That this is a correct division, we can see in a moment by applying it to any great piece of oratory in ancient or modern times. For instance, take the speech of Antony over the body of Julius Cæsar, as imagined by Shakespeare,—here the orator's first object evidently is to inspire belief in himself as "a plain, blunt man," with no ulterior purposes, merely devoted to his friend, bewildered by the death of that friend, unable to understand how confessedly "honourable" men should have brought it about. Accordingly, in the first pause of the speech the citizens say to each other :—

"*2d Cit.* Poor soul! his eyes are red as fire with weeping.
3d Cit. There's not a nobler man in Rome than Antony."

The second object is to produce in the hearers a frame of mind favourable to the designs of the orator, who accordingly awakens in them the passions of gratitude and love towards the memory of Cæsar by the recital of his good deeds, then leads them on to pity and indignation at the thought of the injustice done to him, and finally rouses them to horror and rage by the actual sight of his wounded corpse. Besides this assumption of a particular character, and these appeals to the passions, there are intellectual arguments running through the speech, to the effect that Cæsar was unjustly accused of ambition, and unjustly put to death. And the practical conclusion is urged on the hearers by all these various means—that they should rise in revolt and avenge the death of Cæsar upon his murderers.

This imaginary speech belongs, of course, to the class of deliberative oratory, the object of which is to recommend some course of action. This kind, says Aristotle, deals with the future; while judicial oratory, in criminal or civil cases, endeavours to give a certain complexion to the transactions of the past. And there is a third kind, the oratory of display, which, in proposing toasts and the like, deals chiefly in descriptions of the present. In each of the three kinds of oratory, the three "sources of persuasion" above noted, must be employed. But in order to exhibit the features of a particular character the orator must know the moral nature of man in its various phases; and, in order to work upon the feelings, he must know, so to speak, the inner anatomy of the feelings. A knowledge of human nature is, of course, essential for producing persuasion in the minds of men, and <u>Aristotle thus says that Rhetoric is a compound of Logic and Moral Philosophy</u>. In this treatise he supplies a rich fund of psychological remarks on the various passions and characteristics of men. In the condensed knowledge of the world which it displays the 'Rhetoric' might be compared with Bacon's 'Essays.' It might be compared also with them in this respect—that <u>a bad and Machiavellian use might certainly be made of some of the suggestions which it contains</u>, though Aristotle professes to give them solely to be used in the cause of truth and justice.

With regard to the third "source of persuasion "— the arguments used by an orator must not be scientific demonstrations, nor even dialectical syllogisms, but rhetorical arguments, such as the conditions and circumstances of oratory will admit. For the orator is not like the scientific demonstrator before his pupils, nor is he like the dialectician with his respondent, who will grant him the premises of his argument. The orator has to address a crowd of listeners, with whom as yet he is not in relation; he has to catch, without fatiguing, their attention, and to suggest conclusions without going through every step of the inference. All reasoning, however, must be either inductive or deductive, and the arguments of Rhetoric must each belong to one of these two forms. Aristotle, adapting special names for the purpose, says that the *enthymeme* of Rhetoric answers to the syllogism of Logic, and that the *example* of Rhetoric answers to the induction of Logic.

The word "enthymeme" seems to mean etymologically "a putting into one's mind," or "a suggestion." It is a rhetorical syllogism with premisses constructed out of "likelihoods," or "signs." Some critics consider that it was essential to the "enthymeme" to have one of its premisses suppressed; but Aristotle only says ('Rhet.' I. ii. 13) that this was frequently the case. The real characteristic of the "enthymeme" was its suggestive, but non-conclusive, character; for the premisses, even if expressed in full, would not be sufficient to enforce the conclusion which is pointed at. The "enthymeme" argues either from a "likelihood," that is—a cause which might produce a given effect, though it is not certain to do so; or else from a "sign," that is—an effect which might have been produced by a given cause, though it might also have been produced by something else. To prove that A murdered B, you may argue from the "likelihood" that he would do so, because he was known to have been at feud with him; or from the "sign" that A had blood upon him. Let us observe some of the "enthymemes" in the speech of Antony:—

(1.) "He hath brought many captives home to Rome,
       Whose ransoms did the general coffers fill:
       Did this in Cæsar seem ambitious?
(2.) When that the poor have cried, Cæsar hath wept;
       Ambition should be made of sterner stuff.
(3.) You all did see, that on the Lupercal
       I thrice presented him a kingly crown,
       Which he did thrice refuse. Was this ambition?"

These three arguments are based on "signs;" acts of Cæsar are adduced as showing in him a disinterestedness, a tenderness of heart, and a modesty which would be incompatible with selfish ambition. But the reasoning is not conclusive, since the acts mentioned might have flowed from other sources than good qualities of the heart—they might have been done "with a motive." However, there is fully as much cogency here as can ordinarily be expected to be found in the deductions of an orator. The only inductive reasoning of which oratory is capable is the "example," or historical instance. Instead of gathering sufficient instances to establish a law, which would be the scientific method, <u>the orator quotes one instance pointing in the direction of a law</u>. Thus "Dionysius, in asking to be allowed a body-guard, aims at establishing a tyranny;—did not Pisistratus do just the same?" The "example" is, of course, an arguing by analogy, and the question must always be whether the cases compared with each other are really analogous, or whether there is any essential difference in the circumstances. Aristotle says that some orators deal more in examples, others more in enthymemes. He is inclined to think that in obtaining applause the enthymemes are the more successful.

After thus setting forth the general framework of oratory, Aristotle proceeds to make suggestions with regard to the matter of speeches. This will naturally be different in kind for the three different kinds of oratory. Him who is to practise deliberative oratory, Aristotle advises to study and make himself well acquainted with five points relative to the State to which he belongs: its finance; its foreign relations; the state of its defences; its imports and exports; and its system of law.* In reference to the last of these, Aristotle recommends the comparative study of political constitutions, and for that end that the accounts of travellers should be read. He adds that for political debate in general a knowledge of the works of historians is a valuable preparation.

These, however, are mere hints, directing the student to funds of information which lie outside of the art of

* The same points are specified in the advice given by Socrates to a young politician—Xenophon 'Memorab.' iii. 6.

Rhetoric. Aristotle proceeds to furnish the orator with definitions and theories which he considered (at all events when he was writing this treatise) to belong to Rhetoric itself, though it would have perhaps been a better classification of science if he had merely indicated that a knowledge of these matters was necessary, and had referred the student to Moral Philosophy for full particulars with regard to them. The result is that he gives a brilliant summary by anticipation of a considerable portion of his 'Ethics.' As in the 'Topics' he thought it necessary to make long lists of commonplaces for the use of the dialectician, so here he gives lists of heads to be borne in mind by the deliberative orator. It is not necessary for us to follow Aristotle in anticipating his theory of morals. It need only be mentioned that, after premising that the idea of obtaining personal good, or happiness, is what actuates men in deliberation, —he proceeds to give what may be called a provisional theory of happiness and its component parts; he then specifies thirty different grounds on which a thing might be recommended as good, and forty other grounds upon which a thing might be shown to be comparatively good, or better than something else. He winds up his instructions for the deliberative orator with brief remarks on the scope and character of different forms of government, which are afterwards fully expanded in the 'Politics.'

The oratory of display deals especially with praise and eulogy, as we know from the specimens of it most familiar to us—the funeral oration, and the postprandial speech. The orator in this kind must have before him a clear idea of what constitutes virtue, and of what is, or is considered, most honourable among men. And for his benefit Aristotle inserts a chapter on these subjects, though they more properly belong to moral science. He adds, however, some hints on the rhetorical device of amplification in laudatory, or other, statements. He appends the remark that a knowledge of the theory of virtue is necessary for the deliberative orator also, for the purposes of exhortation and advice. He thus would evidently class hortative addresses, like the modern sermon, under the head of deliberative oratory.

For the use of the forensic orator, who has to argue in accusation or defence, the following equipment of knowledge is provided by Aristotle: 1st, A brief summary of the motives of human action; 2d, An analytical account of pleasure and things pleasurable—for these figure most prominently among human motives; 3d, An analysis of the moods of mind in which men commit injustice; 4th, A distinction between different kinds of law and right; 5th, Remarks on degrees of guilt; and, 6th, Hints for dealing with statutes, documents, and the evidence of witnesses whether these be for or against the orator. Under the 4th head, Aristotle has some fine remarks on the universal law of nature, and on equity.* As a specimen the latter may be quoted:—

"It is equity to pardon human feelings, and to look

* *Epieikeia*, — that quality which Mr Matthew Arnold defines as "a sweet reasonableness."

to the lawgiver, and not to the law; to the spirit, and not to the letter; to the intention, and not to the action; to the whole, and not to the part; to the character of the actor in the long-run, and not in the present moment;—to remember good rather than evil, and good that one has received, rather than good that one has done; to bear being injured; to wish to settle a matter by words rather than by deeds; lastly, to prefer arbitration to judgment, for the arbitrator sees what is equitable, but the judge only the law, and for this an arbitrator was first appointed, in order that equity might flourish."

So much for the materials of oratory. In making use of them, it will be further necessary for the orator to be acquainted with the leading passions and dispositions of men, in order that he may successfully appeal to the feelings of his hearers. Accordingly, the second book of the 'Rhetoric' supplies him with a treatise on the characteristics of Anger, Placability, Friendliness, Hatred, Fear, Shame, Gratitude, Pity, Indignation, Envy, and Emulation; of the three stages of human life—Youth, Maturity, and Old Age; and of the three social conditions—Rank, Wealth, and Power. In these disquisitions there is, probably, embodied much of the collective wisdom of Greece; but there is, doubtless, also a great deal of original analysis, worked out by Aristotle himself once for all, and which has remained valid ever since. Such, for instance, are his six points of contrast between Anger and Hatred ('Rhet.' II. iv. 30) :—

"1st, Anger rises out of something personal to ourselves; Hatred is independent of this. We may hate a man merely because we conceive him to be of a certain description. 2d, Anger is invariably against individuals; Hatred may embrace whole classes. 3d, Anger is to be remedied by time; Hatred is incurable. 4th, Anger wishes to inflict pain, so that its operation may be felt and acknowledged, and thus satisfaction obtained; Hatred wishes nothing of this kind — it merely wishes that a mischief may be done, without caring that the source of it be known. 5th, Anger is a painful feeling; but Hatred not. 6th, Anger, when a certain amount of pain has been inflicted upon its object, may easily turn into pity; Hatred, under all circumstances, is incapable of this,—it desires nothing less than the absolute destruction and non-existence of its object."

With all his subtlety and knowledge of the world, Aristotle does not exhibit any of the cynicism of Hobbes or Rochefoucauld. He is far from denying the existence of disinterested and noble feelings. Thus, for instance, he defines friendly feeling to consist in "the wishing a person what we think good, for his sake and not for our own, and as far as is in our power, the exerting ourselves to procure it." Pity he defines to be "a sort of pain occasioned by the appearance of a hurtful or destructive ill (such as one's self or one's connections might possibly have to endure) happening to one who does not deserve it." Here fellow-feeling is mentioned as necessary for realising the ills which excite our pity, but that by no means reduces pity to a mere selfish apprehension on our own account. "The essence of pity," says Aristotle elsewhere ('Poet.' xxv.), "is that it is caused by the sight of *undeserved* calamity." Thus it proceeds from a sense of moral justice arising in the heart. Aristotle does not regard men as the natural enemies of each other; on the contrary, he thinks benevolent feelings to be natural, and to play a considerable part in the organisation of society. He defines "kindness"* to be "that quality by which one does a service to him who needs it, not in return for anything, nor in order that one may get anything one's self, but simply to benefit the recipient." He considers human nature to be capable of great moral elevation in the persons of the wise and good; at the same time he regarded the majority of mankind as poor creatures, though rather weak than wicked. Thus ('Rhet.' II. v. 7), he says, "the majority of men are timid and corruptible," and in 'Eth.' VII. vii. 1, it is said that "most men are in a state between continence and incontinence, but rather verging towards the worse side."

We may conclude our extracts from the second book of the 'Rhetoric' with Aristotle's remark on the prime of life, which Dr Arnold of Rugby used to be fond of

---

* *Charis*, a word which can hardly be translated, as it means not only kindness, grace, or favour, but also the reciprocal feeling of gratitude for kindness. The *Charites* or Graces were the Greek personifications of reciprocal feelings of kindness. Hence the temple of the Graces symbolised the mutual services of men to each other, on which society depends (see 'Eth.' V. v. 7).

quoting: "The body," says Aristotle, "is in its prime from the age of thirty to thirty-five, and the mind about the age of forty-nine." It has been observed that university undergraduates are apt to consider these ages as set too high, while senior tutors have been known to complain of them as only applicable to precocious southern nations.

From what we have indicated it will be seen that the <u>first two books of the 'Rhetoric' consist mainly of observations on human nature</u>. Towards the close of them Aristotle fell upon the subject of fallacious "enthymemes," and this led him to suspend the work he had in hand, and to write that treatise on "Sophistical Confutations," or "Fallacies," of which we have already given an account. After which he wrote his 'Ethics,' until the subject of "Justice" turned up, and he then went on to discuss the bases of this quality in his 'Politics.' The subject of "Education" seems to have led Aristotle off from the completion of the last-named treatise to write his 'Art of Poetry,' which naturally involved the discussion of rules of style; and this, by an equally natural transition, suggested the completion of the 'Rhetoric,' by the addition of a third book on Style and Arrangement.

This book has of course not quite so universal an interest as the former ones. The interest attaching to it is necessarily to some extent antiquarian—as, for instance, when Aristotle details the five points on which an idiomatic style in Greek depends,—viz., a proper use of connective particles; and of specially appropriate instead of general words; constructing the sentence so as to avoid ambiguity; using right genders; and right numbers. The specification of the latter points (as well as similar injunctions in the 'Art of Poetry') show in how infantile a condition the science of Grammar was in Aristotle's time. He lays down here some of the things which "every schoolboy knows."

The book is not only a good deal limited to the instruction of Greek readers belonging to the fourth century B.C., but it also deals a good deal in allusions which such readers would perfectly understand, but which are obscure for us. Instead of quoting at some length the beauties of oratory, it frequently indicates passages by merely mentioning a single word out of them. There is generally speaking an air of scientific dryness in its treatment even of the most poetical metaphors. For instance, we are told that it is far better to call Aurora the "rosy-fingered" than the "purple-fingered," and still more so than to call her the "red-fingered." But charms of style from the Greek writers appear in this book like moths and butterflies pinned on to corks in the collection of an entomologist. Aristotle's fondness for classification seems carried too far here; he incessantly analyses and enumerates, as for instance when he tells us that there are four ways by which "flatness" in a speech is produced. The principles laid down are of course sound and sensible—as, for example, that "the chief merit of style is clearness," that the orator must not use poetical language, and that his sentences must be rhythmical, without falling into metre. Aristotle objects to having a sentence ended with a short syllable, because the voice cannot rest on it so as to mark a stop; he thinks that the end of each sentence should be marked out by the rhythm, so as not to need punctuation. He recommends the use of the *pæon*, a foot consisting of three short syllables and one long syllable (as ănăchrŏnĭsm), for the rhythmical finish of sentences. The point, however, is not gone into with any exactness; and we are left in doubt as to the proportion which accent bore to "quantity" in ancient Greek oratory. On the one hand we know that accent has had such a firm hold on the Greek language as in the course of time utterly to overpower and eliminate quantity. Thus modern Greek is spoken entirely according to accent without regard to quantity. On the other hand ancient Greek poetry must have been read almost entirely in reference to the quantity of the syllables, without regard to accent. How it stood with ancient Greek rhythmical prose, is a question which Aristotle does not help us to solve. In fact there is a certain matter-of-fact bluntness, and a want of the delicacy and humour of genius, pervading his criticisms. And it is remarkable that his illustrations are more drawn from poetry than from prose—apparently more from books than from living sources,—and that he never mentions with appreciation the oratory of Demosthenes. Some of the greatest speeches of Demosthenes, especially his Olynthiac orations, had been spoken at Athens when Aristotle was little more than thirty years of age, just about the time when he was attempting to rival Isocrates in the teaching of Rhetoric.

It would be extraordinary if these splendid harangues made no impression upon him. But it must be observed that he does not pass any general criticism upon Pericles, or any other orator. And it is possible also that a fear of offending the Macedonian royal family may have prevented Aristotle from praising the anti-Macedonian statesman, though he was the greatest orator among the ancients.

After treating of style, Aristotle briefly discusses arrangement. He divides a speech into exordium, statement, proof, and peroration, and says something on the points to be aimed at in each. He adds some shrewd advice on the use that may be made of putting adroit questions to an opponent; and he mentions with approval the maxim of Gorgias that "when your adversary is earnest you should silence him with ridicule, and when he tries ridicule you should silence him with earnestness." He neatly winds up his 'Rhetoric' with the specimen of a peroration: "I have spoken—you have heard. You have the matter before you—judge of it."

Aristotle's little treatise called 'Poetic,' or the 'Art of Poetry,' is very interesting, but it does not take the modern or romantic view of Poetry. Aristotle does not seek to find here—

> "The light that never was, on sea or land,
> The consecration, and the Poet's dream."

He simply defines poetry as one of the imitative arts, "such as dancing, flute-playing, painting," &c.: these different arts, he says, have each their own instrument of imitation, and poetry uses words and metre. However, not all metrical composition is poetry; the verses of Empedocles are philosophy rather than poetry,—they lack the quality of being imitative, —that is to say, it is not their chief object to depict. Aristotle attributes the *genesis* of poetry, not to any divine impulse, but to those imitative instincts of man, which are exhibited from earliest childhood, and to the intellectual pleasure which we feel in seeing a good imitation even of a painful subject, and in recognising that "*this* is *that*." Poetry then is imitation, and according to this theory the merit of a good poem would be the same as the merit of a good photograph, —exact and mechanical resemblance. Aristotle, however, is not consistent to this view; he evidently admits the idea of some creativeness in the poet,— for instance, he says that some poets represent men as better than they really are; and he applauds the practice of Zeuxis, who, in painting his Helen, combined the beauties out of several fair faces. He seems to approach the modern point of view when he says (xvii. 2) that "Poetry is the province of a genius or a madman;" for the one can feign and the other feels stormy passions. But it must be observed that the word for "a genius" here, is merely "well-natured" —a word elsewhere used for one who has a good moral disposition, and generally for one who has natural gifts. In fact, the philosophy of the imagination was a part of psychology not at all worked out in the time of Aristotle; there was as yet no word to express what we mean by "imagination." When Aristotle uses the word *phantasia*, he means by it, not the creative faculty, but an image before the mind's eye. While the Greeks were the most imaginative of peoples, they had not as yet analysed the processes of imagination. And the want of a terminology connected with this subject is felt throughout the 'Poetic' of Aristotle.

Poetry consists in imitation, mainly of the actions of men; and there are three great species of it—Epic poetry, Tragedy, and Comedy. Of these three kinds Aristotle undertakes to treat; but the promise is only fulfilled with regard to the two first; the treatise breaks off at the point where a disquisition on Comedy might have been expected. Comedy, according to modern views, would hardly be reckoned to be poetry at all. Aristotle, in stating what Comedy is, gives his famous definition of the "ludicrous." Tragedy, he says, aims at representing men who are above the average; comedy, men who are below it. But the characters in comedy are not so much morally bad, as ugly. There is a certain pleasure derivable from ugliness, and that is the sense of the ludicrous. "The ludicrous is some fault or blemish not suggesting the idea of pain or death; as, for instance, an ugly twisted face is ludicrous, if there is no idea that the owner of it is in pain." This saying has been the foundation of all subsequent philosophy of laughter. Elsewhere Aristotle defines the ludicrous as "harmless incongruity." We laugh from a pleasurable sense of contrast and surprise when a thing is out of place but no serious evil seems likely to result.

Aristotle's account of Tragedy is a profound piece of æsthetic philosophy. By implication he defends Tragedy against Plato, who had wished to banish the drama from his ideal republic, as tending to make men unmanly. Aristotle defines Tragedy as the "imitation of some noble action, great and complete in itself; in melodious diction; with different measures to suit the different parts; by men acting, and not by narration; effecting through pity and fear the purging of such feelings." The latter words contain the office and the justification of Tragedy. Men's minds are prone to be haunted by the feelings of pity and fear, and these are apt to degenerate into sentimentality. Tragedy offers noble objects whereon these feelings may be exercised; and by that exercise the feelings not only receive a right direction, but also are relieved, being removed, so to speak, for the time from the system. After much discussion * on the subject in Germany, there is now no doubt that in using the term "purging" in the above passage Aristotle was employing a medical metaphor. This is borne out by two passages of the 'Politics' (II. vii. 11; VIII. vii. 5), which both refer in similar terms to the relief of the passions procured by indulging them. He promised a fuller explanation of his theory on this subject, but unfortunately has never given it. However, we are perhaps safe in understanding that, while Plato objected to Tragedy as tending to make men soft by the excitement of their sympathetic feelings, Aristotle said "No—those feelings

* See 'Aristotle über Kunst, besonders über Tragödie,' von Dr Reinkens (Vienna, 1870), p. 70-167.

will be purged and carried off from the system by the operation of Tragedy."

As to the means by which Tragedy is to excite pity and terror, Aristotle says that it will not do to exhibit a purely good man falling into adversity—that would be rather horrible than tragic; nor, on the other hand, would the representation of a villain receiving the retribution due to his crimes be a tragical story, however moral it might be. We require the element of undeserved calamity; and yet there must be some justice, too, in the course of events, so that, while we feel sorrow for what occurs, we shall feel also that things could not have been otherwise. The tale of Œdipus is often mentioned by Aristotle as a perfect subject for Tragedy. We may add that Mr Tennyson's 'Harold' exhibits in this respect the same qualities; we see in it a noble character borne along to an undeserved and calamitous doom; and yet there is a sense that this is, partly at all events, the result of his own doing. Aristotle is not in favour of a tragedy ending happily. He says that poets sometimes make happy endings out of concession to the weakness of the spectators, but that this is quite a mistake, and that such endings are more suitable to comedy. He praises Euripides as the "most tragic of the poets," on account of the doleful terminations of his plays, "though in other respects he did not manage well."

Much stress has been laid, especially by the French, on "the unities" of the drama, as supposed to be prescribed by Aristotle's 'Poetic.' But in reality he attaches no importance to the external unities of time and place. In enumerating the differences between tragedy and epic poetry, he says (v. 8) that "the one generally tries to limit its action to a period of twenty-four hours, or not much to exceed that, while the other is unlimited in point of time." But he does not lay this down as a law for Tragedy. The peculiarity of the Greek drama, in which a chorus remained constantly present and the curtain never fell, almost necessitated "the unities;" but Aristotle only concerns himself with internal unity, which he says (viii. 4) that Tragedy must have, in common with every other work of art, and which consists in making every part bear an organic relation to the whole, so that no part could be altered or omitted without the whole suffering. This principle, far more valuable than that of "the unities," would seem to need reassertion, for we might almost say that it is habitually violated by writers of fiction in the present day,—at all events by all but the very few who may be placed in the first class.

The 'Poetic' gives many notices of the rise and progress of the Greek drama, and the modifications which tragedy and comedy went through, and much information as to the technical divisions of a play, and other such matters; but all these points have become the property of manuals of "Greek Antiquities." Aristotle notes a decadence of the drama in his own day: he complains of authors spoiling their plays by introducing-episodes merely to suit particular actors: he considers that *spectacle* is carried too far, and that it is a mistake to aim at producing tragical effect by elaborate and expensive scenery and apparatus: he also thinks that acting is overdone. Aristotle shows an extensive acquaintance with dramatic literature; and, by mentioning it, he makes us regret the loss of 'The Flower,' a play by Agathon, which seems to have been entirely original, and not based on any traditional story.

The remarks here made on Epic poetry are comparatively brief. Aristotle considers it of less importance than Tragedy. He says that every merit which the Epic possesses is to be found in Tragedy. Like Tragedy, the Epic must possess unity of plot, but it may indulge to a greater extent in episodes. Aristotle never loses an opportunity of praising Homer, whom he considers to be the author, not only of the 'Iliad' and 'Odyssey,' but also of a comic poem called 'Margites.' He especially commends the art of Homer in making the action of the 'Iliad' and 'Odyssey' respectively circle round definite central events. Although it is a narrative, Epic poetry will always be distinct from history: the one has an artistic unity which is wanting to the other; the one describes what might have been, the other what has been; the one deals in universal, the other in particular, truth. The result of this whole comparison is, that "Poetry is more philosophical and more earnest than History."

The 'Poetic' branches off, towards its close, into an immature disquisition on style, which led Aristotle to go back to his 'Rhetoric,' and write the third book thereof. Here he even lays down some of the elements of grammar, and enumerates the parts of speech. He adds a curious chapter (xxv.) on Criticisms, and how to answer them, in which the spirit of the dialectician is very apparent. All this shows that Aristotle was only gradually feeling his way to the division of sciences. He wrote, as it were, under pressure, on one great subject after another, and the light only dawned on him as he went along. Could he have rewritten his works, probably all would have been brought into lucid order. But it is clear that the little treatise called 'Poetic' not only was never rewritten, but was never finished as its author intended it to be.

CHAPTER V.

ARISTOTLE'S 'ETHICS.'

ARISTOTLE's treatise on Morals has come down to us entitled 'Nicomachean Ethics.' This label was probably affixed to the work on account of Nicomachus, the son of Aristotle, having had some subordinate connection with it, either as scribe or editor; and in order to distinguish it in the Peripatetic library from the 'Eudemian Ethics,' which is a sort of paraphrase of Aristotle's treatise by his disciple Eudemus,—and from the 'Great Ethics' which is a restatement of the same matter by some later Peripatetic hand. Among the Works of Aristotle there is also included a little tract 'On Virtues and Vices.' This is a mere paper, such as the Peripatetic school used to produce, noting characteristics of some of the Aristotelian good qualities and their opposites, and with no pretensions to be considered genuine.

After going through, under the guidance of Aristotle, the theory of the reasonings by which knowledge is obtained, and the theory of the statement by which knowledge may be best set forth, we now enter, in the 'Nicomachean Ethics,' upon some of the matter of knowledge—namely, Aristotle's theory of human life. But what strikes us on reading the early chapters of this treatise is that, when he began to write it, Aristotle had no clear conception of the existence of Moral Philosophy as a separate science. The question which he proposes is, What is the end, or supreme good, aimed at by human action? He adds that the science which will have to settle this will be a branch of Politics—that is, of State-philosophy;—for the chief good of the State and of the individual are identical, only the one is on a grander scale than the other. In this exordium we may notice two especially Greek features : *first*, the cardinal question proposed for the philosophy of human life is not, What is the duty of man? but, What is the chief good for man? *Secondly*, the individual is so far subordinated to and identified with the State, that the *summum bonum* for the latter includes that of the former. In Aristotle's 'Politics' (VII. iii. 8), the chief good for a State is portrayed as consisting in the development and play of speculative thought, all fit conditions thereto having been provided. The idea is —a Greek city, with a slave population doing the hard work, wherein the citizens for the most part can live as gentlemen, and a large proportion of them may devote their lives to intellectual pursuits. Aristotle thought that the highest aim for a State was to turn out philosophers, and that the highest aim for an individual was to be a philosopher. Thus there is a seeming identity of aims; yet still in writing his 'Ethics'

Aristotle confines himself to inquiring after "the good" for the individual. As he goes on, it dawns upon him more and more (see 'Eth.' v. 5-11), that "the man" has an independent status distinct from that of "the citizen," and that in his capacity of human being each citizen has needs, aims, and virtues of his own, irrespective of the State. Thus by composing this work he established the separation of Ethics from Politics,—these two sciences having been previously mixed up together by Socrates and Plato, who were the great founders of both.

What constitutes the chief good for an individual, or in other words, happiness? Aristotle is somewhat abstract and metaphysical in arguing upon this question. He says, happiness must be an end in itself, and not a means to anything else; it must lie within the proper sphere or function of man,—that function being a rational and moral life; it must be, not a merely dormant state, but a state of conscious vitality; and lastly, it must be in accordance with the law of excellence proper to the function of man. Thus we arrive at the general idea that the highest happiness consists in the harmonious exercise of man's highest powers; and the treatise ends by declaring particularly that the speculative reason is man's highest endowment, and that the truest happiness consists in philosophic thought.

"This," he exclaims ('Eth.' X. vii. 7), "would be perfect human happiness, if prolonged through a life of full duration. Such a life, however, would be superhuman; for it is not as being man that one will live thus, but by virtue of a certain divine element subsisting within us. Just as this element far excels our composite nature, so does its operation excel action according to the moral virtues. Reason in comparison with man is something divine, and so is the life of Reason divine in comparison with the routine of man's life. One must not, however, obey those who bid us 'think humbly as being mortal men,' nay rather we should indulge immortal longings, and strive to live up to that divine particle within us, which, though it be small in proportionate bulk, yet in power and dignity far surpasses all the other parts of our nature, and which is indeed each man's proper self. By living in accordance with it our true individuality will be developed. And such a life cannot fail to be happy above all other kinds of life."

This, then, is the "mark" which Aristotle sets before men to "shoot at" ('Eth.' I. ii. 2)—namely, the attainment of a state in which one should live above the world, occupied with philosophic thought. It is an ideal picture, to which, however, approximations may doubtless be made. To attain it completely would be, according to Aristotle, to attain the life of the blessed existences, such as the sun and the fixed stars, and of God Himself, whose essence is Reason, and His life "a thinking upon thought" ('Met.' XI. ix. 4). This, he admits, is impossible for us; but yet, he says, we should aim at it. "Secondary to this," he says, "in point of happiness, is the life of moral virtue."

And here we must notice the peculiar way in which the idea of "virtue" is introduced into the 'Ethics.' Instead of at once recognising the law of moral obligation as the deepest thing in man, Aristotle, as we have seen above, introduces the idea of virtue and morality in a dry logical way, saying that the chief good for man must consist in the realisation of his powers "according to their own proper law of excellence." Having in this colourless and neutral way brought in the term "excellence" or virtue, Aristotle divides it, in relation to man, into moral and intellectual. Of the former he proceeded immediately to treat at length; of the latter he promised to give an account, but only an imperfect realisation of that promise, furnished by the "Eudemian" paraphrase, has come down to us.

Both by the way in which it is introduced, and the terms in which it is finally dismissed ('Eth.' X. viii. 1), the moral nature of man is made to hold a subsidiary place in Aristotle's 'Ethics.' Yet still we find that almost all the treatise is taken up with discussions directly or indirectly concerning the practical and moral nature. And thus Aristotle, groping his way in a science which had as yet no distinct landmarks, contributed much towards the subsequent deeper conception of ethical questions. One service which he performed was to distinguish will from reason. Socrates and Plato had been content to describe virtue as knowledge, or an enlightened state of the reason; but Aristotle, like Kant in modern times, defined it as a state of the will. Secondly, he analysed the formation of this state, and explained it by his doctrine of "habits." By observing the various arts—as, for instance, harp-playing, and the like—he saw that "practice makes perfect;" and concluded that as by playing the harp a man became a harp-player, so by doing just things a man would become just, by doing brave things he would become brave; and, in short, that actions have a tendency to reproduce themselves, and thus to produce habits or states of the will. All this is trite enough now, but it was formulated for the first time by Aristotle.

In laying down his famous doctrine that it is the characteristic of virtue to preserve "the mean," Aristotle was not entirely original. In this, as in many other cases, he only fixed into scientific form a conception which had been previously floating in the mind of Greece. Hesiod, the Seven Sages, the unknown authors of 'Maxims,' the Gnomic poets, Pindar, and the Tragedians, had all preached the doctrine of moderation—a doctrine most congenial to the natural good taste of the Hellenic people, who instinctively despised excess in any form as unintellectual and barbarous. What had hitherto been a universal popular *dictum*, Plato raised into philosophy, by pointing out ('Philebus,' p. 23-27) that in all things the law of "limit" is the cause of good, while the unlimited, the unregulated, the chaotic—is evil. Thus, in the human body, the unlimited is the tendency to extremes, to disorder, to disease; but the introduction of the limit produces a balance of the constitution and good health. In sounds you have the infinite degrees of deep and high, quick and slow; but the limit gives rise to modulation and harmony, and all that is delightful in music. In climate and temperature, where the limit has been introduced, excessive heats and violent storms subside, and the mild and genial seasons in their order follow. In the human mind "the goddess of the limit" checks into submission the wild and wanton passions, and gives rise to all that is good. Thus, in contemplating all things, whether physical or moral, there was present to the mind of Plato the same train of associations,—the same ideas of measure, proportion, balance, harmony, moderation, and the like. Elsewhere ('Republic,' p. 400) he dwells especially on the common characteristics of art and morality, pointing out that measure and symmetry are the causes of excellence in both alike. Aristotle took over these thoroughly Greek ideas from Plato, and adapted them to his own purpose. He slightly changed the mode of expression: instead of "moderation" he introduced a mathematical term, "the mean" (for instance, 4 is the mean between 2 and 6); he used this term as the chief feature in a regular formal definition of moral virtue; and he drew out a table of the virtues showing that each of them was a mean between two extremes. Thus the virtue Courage lies between the vice Cowardice, which is fearing too much, and the vice Rashness, which is fearing too little. And virtue generally is a balance between too much and too little. It is produced by the introduction of the law of the mean into the passions, which in themselves are unlimited. But what is this "mean"—this *juste milieu*

—and how is it ascertained? Aristotle tells us that it is not merely the mid-point between two external quantities, but it is the mid-point relatively to the moral agent. What is too much for one man—say, of danger, expense, indulgence, or self-valuation—may be by no means too much for another man. The moral mean is thus a fluctuating quantity, dependent on considerations of the person and the moment. To hit upon it exactly requires a fine tact, for "virtue is more nice and delicate than the finest of the fine arts" ('Eth.' II. vi. 9). This tact, or sense of moral beauty, we have by nature ('Politics,' I. ii. 12); but it only exists in perfection, after cultivation by experience, in the mind of the wise man, and to him in all cases must be the ultimate appeal.

Objection has been raised in modern times to the theory of Aristotle, on the ground that it makes only a quantitative difference between virtue and vice. A little more or a little less does not seem to us to constitute the whole difference which subsists between "right" and "wrong." But we must remember that the Greeks did not speak of actions as "right" or "wrong," but as "beautiful" and "ugly." From this point of view each action was looked upon as a work of art; and as in art and literature, so in morals, the great aim was to avoid the "too much" and the "too little," and thus to attain perfection. This idea of beauty and grace in action pervaded the Hellenic life, and good taste seemed to stand in the place of conscience. To attain "the beautiful" is considered by Aristotle, if inferior to the joys of philosophy, still as a source of very high gratification; and he describes the brave man ('Eth.' III. ix. 4) as consciously meeting death in a good cause, and consciously sacrificing a happy life, full of objects which he holds dear, because by so doing he attains "the beautiful." If we ask, however, what constituted the beauty of this act? Aristotle's doctrine can only tell us that the brave man dared and feared neither too much nor too little, but in the proper degree and manner, considering the circumstances of the moment. These *formulæ*, however, do not appear to explain what we should consider the moral beauty of the act in question. We should rather point to the self-sacrifice of the act; the spectacle of an individual preferring to his own life the good of others, the defence of his country, the maintenance of some noble cause—as what was beautiful and touching. "The mean" may serve as a general expression for the law of artistic beauty, but it seems not deep enough to express what we prize most in human action.

Aristotle's table of the virtues does not, of course, comprise the Christian qualities of humility, charity, chastity, self-devotion, and the like. It even falls short of the summary of human excellence given by Plato in his enumeration of the five cardinal virtues ('Protag.,' p. 349)—courage, temperance, justice, wisdom, and holiness. Aristotle separates ethics from religion, and thus leaves out all consideration of "holiness," or man's conduct in relation to God. "Wisdom" and "Justice" he reserves to be made the subject of separate discussions: the one as being an excellence of the intellect, and not a "mean state" of the passions; the other as being dependent on, and mixed up with, all the institututions of the State. The table, then, thus restricted, contains the names of nine or ten good qualities, such as would adorn the character of a perfect Grecian gentleman. They are Courage; Temperance; Liberality; Magnificence (liberality on a larger scale); Magnanimity, or Great-souledness; Self-respect (the same on a smaller scale); Mildness; Wit; Truthfulness of manner; and Friendliness. And the pairs of extremes which respectively environ each of these "mean states" are specified, in some cases names being invented for them. The most moral of the virtues here named, from a modern point of view, is Courage, on account of the self-sacrifice, the endurance of danger, pain, and death, which it implies. Temperance is far from being represented by Aristotle as an utter self-abnegation; he says (III. xi. 8) that the temperate man, with due regard to his health, and to the means at his disposal, and acting under the law of the beautiful, will preserve a balance in regard to the pleasures of sense. Aristotle loves the virtues of Liberality and Magnificence (the latter meaning tasteful outlay on great objects) on account of their brilliancy. He undervalues the virtue of saving, and erroneously considers that parsimony does more harm than spendthrift waste. He describes Magnanimity by drawing a fancy portrait of the "Great-souled man." Such a man has all the Aristotelian virtues; he is great and superior to other men, and has a corresponding loftiness of soul. He will not compete for the common objects of ambition; he will only attempt great and important matters, and otherwise will seem inactive;

he will be open in friendship and hatred, really straightforward and deeply truthful, but reserved and ironical in manner to common people. He will live for his friend alone, will wonder at nothing, will bear no malice, will be no gossip, will not be anxious about trifles, will care more to possess that which is beautiful than that which is profitable. His movements are slow, his voice is deep, and his diction is stately.

The four last virtues in the table are qualities to adorn the external man in society, and as such seem more worthy of a place in Lord Chesterfield's Letters than in a treatise of Moral Philosophy. To be mild without being spiritless; to be friendly without servility; to have a simple manner without either assumption or mock-humility; and to be witty without buffoonery,—these achievements constitute the minor excellences with which Aristotle concludes his list. He was proceeding to show that the law of the mean is exemplified in the instinctive feelings of modesty and virtuous indignation—when, through some unknown cause, his MS broke off ('Eth.' IV. ix. 8) in the middle of a sentence.

What should have followed here was, *first*, a dissertation on the nature of Justice; and, *secondly*, an account of the Intellectual excellences. And it was very important that this part of the work should be adequately executed. Under the head of Justice fell to be considered ('Eth.' IV. vii. 7) the relation of the individual to truth of word and deed. And an adequate account of Justice and of Wisdom might have redeemed Aristotle's previous account of moral virtue from that superficial appearance which it must be said to present. But unfortunately we do not appear to possess at first hand Aristotle's execution of this part of his task. What happened may perhaps have been this: when Aristotle arrived at this point, he put aside the subject of Justice, to be treated after he had written his 'Politics' and had cleared his views on the foundations of Justice in the State. At the same time he put aside the subject of the Intellectual excellences, perhaps till he should have written his 'Metaphysics.' It must be remembered that he kept many parts of his Encyclopædia in course of construction at once, and he would drop one part and take up another, as suited his train of thought. In the present case he did not entirely abandon his 'Ethics,' but went on to write the three last books, merely leaving the centre part to be filled in subsequently. Doubtless the matter for that centre part was expounded to and discussed in the Peripatetic school, but Aristotle probably never himself expressed it in literary form. When, however, Eudemus came to write his paraphrase of the 'Ethics,' he was enabled to fill in the gap which still existed in them by supplying a portion, the matter of which partly came from school notes and partly from Aristotle's other writings, while the language was that of Eudemus himself, continuous with the rest of the paraphrase. Afterwards Nicomachus, or some other editor, took this supplementary piece from the 'Eudemian Ethics' and stuck it in as Books V., VI., VII. of the 'Ethics' of Aristotle.

The theory of Justice which has thus come down to us as Aristotle's, is indistinctly stated in Book V. It seems to be borrowed a good deal from the 'Politics;' it expounds the principles of Justice which exist in the State, and merely defines Justice in the individual as the will to conform to these principles. Thus really no contribution to ethical science is made. It is shown how Justice is manifested (1) in distributions by the State, (2) in correcting wrongs done between man and man, (3) in the ordinary course of commerce. Some first steps in political economy, being remarks on the nature of money, on value, and on price, given in chap. v., are perhaps the most interesting points in this book.

Book VI. appears to be to some extent borrowed from Aristotle's 'Organon' and treatise 'On the Soul.' It is confusedly written, and two questions seem to be mixed up in it: (1) What is the Moral Standard? (2) What are the Intellectual excellences? The former question receives no definite answer; with regard to the latter we are informed that there are two distinct and supremely good modes of the intellect—"Wisdom," which is the culmination of the philosophic reason, and "Thought," which is the perfection of the practical reason. This latter quality forms the main subject of the book. It is described as being developed in combination with the development of the moral will. It is an ideal attribute, and we are told that "he who has 'Thought' possesses all the virtues" ('Eth.' VI. xiii. 6). The distinction here indicated between the practical and philosophic reason was undoubtedly a contribution to psychology first made by Aristotle. It was an improvement upon the views of Plato, and a step towards those of Kant.

Book VII. supplies, in the words of Eudemus, a valuable complement to Aristotle's moral system. It discusses the intermediate states between virtue and vice, and especially analyses the state called "incontinence," or "weakness," as exhibited in the process of yielding to temptation. By aid of the forms of the syllogism it is shown how, while having good principles in our mind, we may fail under temptation to act upon them. On the other hand, the idea is introduced of an ideally vicious man, who has no conscience or remorse, but all his mind is in harmony with the dictates of vice; a conception with which we may compare the character drawn by Shelley in his portrait of Count Cenci. The whole of this book is marked by a phraseology different from and later than that of the genuine parts of the 'Ethics.' It deals much in physiological considerations, and it winds up with a modified paraphrase of Aristotle's treatise on Pleasure, given in Book X.

Books VIII. and IX. treat of Friendship, which "is either a virtue, or is closely connected with virtue;" and no part of the whole treatise is more pleasing or admirable. The idea of friendship has probably always found a place among civilised nations, but it obtained peculiar prominence among the Greeks, partly owing to the subordinate position assigned to women, and the consequent rarity of sympathetic marriages. Among the Dorians, from early times, there had subsisted a custom by which each warrior had attached to him, as his squire, a boy whom he was expected to inspire with becoming thoughts. The one member in this pair was called "the inbreather," the other "the listener." Out of this custom sentimental relationships arose, which Plato approving wrote his famous descriptions of those pure and passionate attachments between persons of the same sex, known as "Platonic love." With this sentimentality Aristotle did not sympathise, but yet there is no coldness in his picture of friendship. He asserts enthusiastically the glow of the heart which is caused by contemplating the actions of a virtuous friend (IX. ix. 5), and declares that without this element in life no one can be called truly happy. Lord Bacon's splendid essay 'Of Friendship' may be compared with these pages; but Bacon's account of the advantages of a friend is on a lower level and less philosophical than that given by Aristotle, who goes to the root of the matter in saying that what a friend really does for you is, by the joint operation of sympathy and contrast, of *quasi* identity and yet diversity—to intensify the sense of your personal existence, and to give you that vividness of vitality on which happiness depends (IX. ix. 7). In this proposition the two books culminate, but they are full of lucid distinctions, and also of high morality. Friendship (as has been seen above, p. 87) is represented by Aristotle as an utterly disinterested feeling, often calling for great self-sacrifice. Sometimes, he says, the good man may be called upon to die for his friends (IX. viii. 9); and as a delicate form of disinterestedness he inquires whether in some cases one ought not to give up to one's friend, instead of seizing for one's self, the opportunity of doing noble actions.

Almost the only matter of any importance in the

'Ethics' of Aristotle which we have not already summarised is his disquisition on Pleasure in Book X. There was a good deal of abstract questioning in the time of Aristotle as to whether Pleasure could be "the chief good," or whether it could be considered a good at all. The Platonists were disposed to be hard upon Pleasure. But all this turned a good deal upon the prior question, "What Pleasure is?" Aristotle showed that an erroneous definition had been taken up by the Platonic school, who considered pleasure to be a sense of restoration,—a sense of our powers, after exhaustion, being brought up to their normal state. Kant has given a very similar definition, saying that "pleasure is the sense of that which promotes life, pain of that which hinders it." Aristotle says that this is wrong; that it applies only to eating and drinking, and such things, and that Pleasure is not "the sense of what promotes life," but the sense of life itself; the sense of the vital powers, the sense that any faculty whatsoever has met its proper object. Pleasure, then, according to the Platonists, was the accompaniment of an imperfect condition, like recovery after illness. According to Aristotle it was, except in the case of certain spurious pleasures, the play and action of that which is healthy in us. From this point of view it is obvious that Pleasure must in itself be a good, and that when it consists in the exercise of the highest faculties (see above, p. 102) it becomes identical with the highest happiness. Lest it be thought that this exaltation of Pleasure might have dangerous results from a moral point of view, we will mention one safeguard which accompanies the Aristotelian doctrine. He tells us that for anything to be "good" in life, it must be an end-in-itself : that is,—something desirable for its own sake, and not as a mere means to something else; something thoroughly worthy, in which the mind can rest satisfied. Thus all mere amusements are excluded from being good, because they are not ends-in-themselves. And this maxim may be deduced from Aristotle : "Act as far as possible so that at any moment you may be able to say to yourself, 'What I am now doing is an end-in-itself.'"

CHAPTER VI.

ARISTOTLE'S 'POLITICS.'

The 'Ethics' of Aristotle end with the words, "Let us then commence our 'Politics.'" He had described virtue and happiness, but neither of these, he says,* is attainable by any human being apart from society. Moral development and the full enjoyment of the exercise of our powers equally demand certain external conditions; they cannot exist save by the aid of a settled community, social habits, the restraint and protection of laws, and even a wisely regulated system of public education. Man is by nature a social creature; he cannot isolate himself without becoming either more or less than man—"either a god or a beast." The state is, therefore, a prime necessity for the "well-doing and well-being" of the individual. In fact, says Aristotle,† you cannot form any conception of man in his normal condition—that is to say, in a civilised condition—except as a member of a state. On these grounds Aristotle proposed to go on to the writing of his 'Politics' as the complement and conclusion of his ethical treatise. But some time probably elapsed before the design was

* 'Eth.' X. x. 8-23.   † 'Pol.' I. ii. 13, 14.

carried out; * and in the interval it is not unreasonable to suppose that Aristotle, seeking, as usual, to base theory upon experience, was engaged in making that remarkable collection called the 'Constitutions' (see above, p. 48), which contained a history and description of no less than 158 states, and of which numerous fragments remain.

However this may be, the 'Politics' forms a rich repertory of facts relating to the history of Greece. And it abounds, too, in the knowledge of human nature, and in wise and penetrating observations on the conduct and motives of mankind, many of which are applicable to all times and countries. The treatise is not entire; it breaks off in the middle of one of the most interesting parts of all, namely Aristotle's theory of education. Perhaps this was one of the cases in which Aristotle, finding that his mind was not fully made up on a particular subject, dropped that subject for the time, meaning to revert to it, but never actually doing so. Besides its unfinished condition, the 'Politics' also shows indications of a certain amount of disarrangement in the order of its books. If re-arranged according to their natural order, the books in Bekker's edition would stand thus :—

Book I. On the Family as a constituent element in the State.

Book II. Containing a criticism of some previous theories about the State, and of some remarkable actual constitutions.

* Spengel, one of the most judicious of German critics, says, that "the 'Politics' was written long after the 'Ethics.'"

Books III., VII., VIII. Giving Aristotle's own conception of an Ideal State,—unfortunately not concluded.

Books IV., VI., V. Forming a return from the ideal point of view to practical statesmanship, and suggesting remedies for different evils apparent in the contemporary Governments of Greece.

It has been well pointed out * that in Aristotle's treatment of the above-mentioned subjects three incongruous elements may be detected: "really scientific inquiry, aristocratic prejudice, and the dreams of a metaphysical philosophy which soars to heaven and listens for the eternal harmonies of nature." The scientific spirit shows itself in the vast apparatus of history which Aristotle employs, his researches into the customs of barbarous tribes, and his careful recognition of the immense variety to be found in constitutions coming under the same general name (such as Democracy, Aristocracy, &c.) when studied according to the peculiar circumstances of each case. All this would constitute his work a contribution to the science of "Comparative Politics."

But another spirit, alien from that of free and inductive inquiry, occasionally manifests itself, especially when Aristotle appeals to "nature" either in defending or attacking any institution. "Nature" is, of course, a rather slippery word: it may mean either of two things, —either "primitive condition," in which sense a savage is in a state of nature; or "normal condition," in which

* Mr A. Lang's Essays on Aristotle's 'Politics,' p. 15 (Longmans, 1877).

sense the most perfectly civilised man has attained his natural state. The latter sense is the one which Aristotle generally has in his mind; he generally means by "nature" the normal and perfect state of things, or a power in the world working towards that normal state. But the question arises, How do we know what is the perfect and normal state of things? Philosophers are too apt to dignify by the name of "nature" any arrangement for which they may have a predilection. And Aristotle cannot be entirely exonerated from having done so. He sometimes attributes a sort of divine right to things as they are, calling them "natural." Thus he treats of the family as "naturally" constituted of man, wife, child, and slave. Certain reformers of the 4th century B.C. had already lifted up their voices against the institution of slavery. They had argued that the slave was of the same flesh and blood as his master, and might be as good as he; and that, in short, slavery was merely an unjust and oppressive custom which mankind could and should alter. But to the mind of Aristotle slavery was a necessary institution in order to provide citizens with that amount of leisure which would enable them to live ideal lives in the pursuit of the true and the beautiful (see above, p. 101). Therefore with unconscious bias he proceeded to argue that slavery was "natural," on the ground that some races of men were by "nature" born to serve, being deficient in that "large discourse" of reason which other men possessed, and which gave them a "natural" right to command. He seeks for external indications of this great difference between man and man, and says that slaves are "barbarians" (*i. e.*, ignorant of the Greek language and Greek manners), and again, that they have not the upright bearing of freemen trained in the gymnasia. But he admits that "nature" has failed in outwardly marking with sufficient distinctness the inward difference between the slave and his master. Yet still he is not shaken in his doctrine, but even asserts that it is lawful to make war on races which were intended by "nature" to be slaves, and to reduce them to slavery. These views may seem shocking; but yet they admit of some palliation. Christian theologians and divines, till within a very recent time, have defended slavery, appealing in its behalf to the sanction of the Bible; and even the virtuous Bishop Berkeley, while sojourning at Rhode Island, became the owner of slaves. The lot of a slave in Attica seems, generally speaking, not to have been a bad one. And Aristotle, in wishing the "naturally" deficient races of mankind to be brought into bondage, seems to have had some idea of the benefit they would derive from being, as it were, sent to school.

In another matter Aristotle appealed to "nature" not in defending, but in attacking, one of the institutions of society—namely, the putting out money at interest. Aristotle had many of the prejudices of a "gentleman;" we have seen before (p. 109) how he admired a brilliant liberality, and thought little of the virtue of saving. He acknowledged that means must be forthcoming for the maintenance of the family, but, if possible, he would have these means come from the produce of the soil,* crops, animals, or minerals, for these sources of support are "natural." With trade and traffic he had no sympathy, but he admitted that practically they must go on; and he said that people who valued success in such things might try and imitate the philosopher Thales, who foresaw, by his astrology, on one occasion, that there would be a great olive harvest, and while it was still winter hired all the olive presses in the country, and when the demand for these set in, was able to get his own terms and realise a large sum, "thus showing that it is easy for philosophers to be rich, if they only cared about it." These contemptuous expressions in regard to commerce clearly indicate that Aristotle did not take a calm intellectual view of the subject; he did not see that it was a subject worthy of being reduced to a science, else he would not have left the doing of this to Adam Smith. Yet still in a book full of the shrewdest remarks on social arrangements we cannot fail to be struck by the antiquated look of the announcement that "lending money on interest is justly abominated, and is the most unnatural of all forms of gain, for it diverts money from its proper purpose (which was to be a mere instrument of exchange) and forces it unnaturally to breed." † This saying of Aristotle's doubtless did something to foster the prejudice against "usury" and Jews, in the latter part of the Middle Ages. The notion is apparently based

* 'Pol.' I. x. 3.

† Compare Shakespeare, 'Merchant of Venice,' Act i. scene 3:—

Antonio. Or is your gold and silver ewes and rams?
Shylock. I cannot tell; I make it breed as fast.

upon the first-mentioned conception of "nature"—as the primitive state of things. "Interest is not a primitive institution, and therefore it is unnatural." The very opposite of this conclusion would be thought true nowadays. We feel now that money unspent "naturally" acquires interest and compound interest, and that in a civilised community nothing is more unnatural than the "talent laid up in a napkin."

An enthusiastic and almost mystical spirit exhibits itself in Aristotle when he discourses on the Ideal State. Having laid it down that Happiness for the state and for the individual is one and the same ('Pol.' VII. ii. 1), he seems for a moment to waver and hesitate as to whether he should not retract the doctrine expressed in the 'Ethics' (see above, p. 102), that the happiness to be found in a life of thought is incomparably superior to that to be found in a life of action. Could this be said of a state—that is, of a whole community? If a whole community is engaged in the fruition of philosophical thought, must they not be isolated from international relations and cut off from the world? But Aristotle does not flinch ultimately from the results of his doctrine. He says ('Pol.' VII. ii. 16) that "it is quite possible that a state may be situated in some isolated position," enjoying good laws and knowing nothing of war or foreign relations, and that in such a state (VII. iii. 8) the community may be engaged in contemplations and thoughts which have their own end in themselves, and do not aim at any external results. As is the life of God or of the conscious universe (each brooding over their own perfections), such will be the life of the Ideal State!

This announcement of the highest end to be aimed at by Politics is as if some modern writer, in treating of the State, should seek to identify it with the Invisible Church of God. Or, again, it may remind us of the saying that the supreme and ultimate product of civilisation is "two or three gentlemen talking together in a room." This paradox is true and quite Aristotelian: mental activities are the highest things of all; enactments, and police, and wars, and treaties exist for the sake of order, of which the best fruit is the mutual play of intelligence and the glow of friendship. But one peculiarity of Aristotle's ideal politics is the comparative smallness of their scale. Like a true Greek, he does not think of nations and empires, but of city-states. It has been said that the city-state was something like the University of modern times. Aristotle regarded it as an organism of limited size, in which every citizen should have his function, and in which every one should be personally known to the rulers. He said ('Eth.' IX. x. iii.) that 100,000 citizens would be far too many to constitute a state. Some of the peculiarities of his Ideal State may be specified as follows:—Every full citizen was to be a landowner, with slaves to cultivate his soil, but no great accumulation of property in any one man's hands was to be allowed. The citizens were to constitute a warrior caste, and were each to be admitted in turn, when of mature age, to a share in the government. No artisan or tradesman was to be a citizen; the city was to have a harbour, but not too near, so as not to be flooded with strangers; the navy was to be manned by slaves; the city itself was, for salubrity, to slope towards the east and to catch the winds of morning. Lastly, the State itself was to be a perfect Sparta in point of discipline, though aiming at something higher than mere gymnastic and military drill. There was to be a common primary instruction for all the citizens from the age of seven to fourteen, and a common secondary instruction from fourteen to twenty-one. The "branches" were to be gymnastic, letters, drawing, and music. Everything was to be taught with a view to culture, rather than to utility. Thus the object of learning drawing was "to make one observant of beauty." In regard to gymnastic, Aristotle wisely warns against a premature strain of the powers, and says that it is very rare for the same person to have won a prize, as a boy, and as a man, at the Olympic games. He lays great stress on the moral and educational influence of music, and its efficacy in "purging" the emotions (see above, p. 95). He disparages pipe-playing, which, he says, was adopted by the Athenians in the glorious period of licence succeeding their victories over the Persians; and adds that "pipe-playing not only disfigures the face, but has nothing intellectual in it." It is difficult for us to enter into many of the feelings of the ancients about music. Aristotle lauds the "Dorian mood;" and here his treatise breaks off, without his having given us his theory as to instruction in literature, or as to the secondary instruction in general of his ideal citizens.

In constructing a Utopia, Aristotle was, of course,

following the example of the celebrated 'Republic' of Plato; but his object was to improve upon the conceptions of his master, whom he criticised with courtesy, but in a prosaic spirit. Plato's "city" avowedly existed in dreamland, but Aristotle applied to it the tests of historical experience and everyday possibility. While accepting the idea of a city of contemplation, Aristotle determined that its institutions should be such as to approve themselves to practical commonsense. The contrast between the two philosophers in this matter is very striking—the one daring, creative, and full of the play of fancy; the other laborious, matter-of-fact, and scientific. It is not certain that Plato's wild suggestions for a community of wives and property were meant to be taken seriously; but Aristotle takes them so, and gives us the first arguments on record against Communism. He defends the institution of property as "natural," and says that "it makes an unspeakable difference in the enjoyment of a thing to feel that it is your own." All his remarks on this point are sagacious; but there is a singular spirit of conservatism shown in his saying ('Pol.' II. v. 16) that "if Plato's notions had been good they would have been adopted long ago." Instead of looking forward to a future of discovery and progress, Aristotle rather looked back, thinking that all perfection had been attained in the past.

In Books IV., VI., V. of his 'Politics' (see above, p. 119), Aristotle turns from the ideal to the actual, and lays down a theory of the different forms of government which are possible, the causes which give rise to these different forms, their respective merits and disadvantages, and the practical means for obviating the evils to which they are respectively exposed. Greek society was very unstable; Athens and many other cities were, like Paris during the last half-century, in chronic expectation of a revolution. Therefore a theory of seditions and revolutions became an essential part of Greek political science, and Aristotle furnishes one accordingly, containing the wise remark that "small things are never the cause, though they are often the occasion, of popular revolt." He shows that there are three normal forms of government,—the Monarchy, or government by one wise ruler; the Aristocracy, or government by a select number of the wisest and best; and the "Constitution," or mixed government, in which democratic, monarchic, and aristocratical elements are balanced against each other. Each of these normal and perfect forms, wherever they have existed, has followed a tendency to diverge into a corruption of itself;—the monarchy degenerates into Tyranny, the aristocracy into Oligarchy, and the "Constitution" into Democracy. These lower forms are the kinds of government which Aristotle practically finds in the world. He shows how each of them is constantly menaced by revolution, and from what special causes, namely, the peculiar jealousies which each is apt to engender. He says that it is not the desire of gain, so much as tenacity of rights or fancied rights, that causes revolution. He gives various pieces of advice to those who administer the different forms of government; —one of which is that each government should avoid emphatically asserting its own special character. The democracy should be as little democratic, the tyrant as little tyrannous, the oligarchy as little exclusive and overbearing as possible,—so that in each case some approach might be made to the golden "mean," which is the true cause of political stability.

In his high appreciation of the "Constitution," or well-mixed government, Aristotle may be thought to have had an unconscious anticipation of the guarded liberties, and of the combination of order with progress, which are the blessing and the pride of England. But in one respect he totally fails to come up to the grandeur of the modern conception; for, as said before, he thinks of arrangements for a city and not for a nation, and he has no idea of those representative institutions by which political freedom of action on a large scale may be provided. As his views for each state were limited, so also he did not take sufficient thought of international relations. For one moment he seemed to have caught a glimpse of possibilities which he might have followed out into important conclusions; for he says ('Pol.' VII. vii. 3) that "owing to the happy moderation of the climate of Greece, the Hellenic race possess a combination of the best qualities which fall to the lot of the human species, being both high-spirited and intellectual; and if they could all together form one political state, the Greeks might govern the world." He drops out this isolated thought, but does not pursue it. At the moment when he was writing, the Hellenic race was in the utmost danger; it was, in fact, doomed to fall from its high position into political extinction, and all for the want of "solidarity," all from these jealousies which kept each Greek city apart from the rest. Aristotle's peculiar relations to the court of Macedon may have hindered him from freely entering upon this subject, or may have biassed his views; but the real fact seems rather to have been that, while he was a great philosopher, he was no statesman, and that, absorbed in the researches of science and in the dreams of an ideal state, he did not see the actual dangers of his country so clearly as his patriotic contemporary Demosthenes saw them. His contribution to politics was abstract and scientific, and as such remains valid for all time; his analysis of the pathology (so to speak) of oligarchies and democracies was found to be often strikingly verified in the history of the Italian republics. And however much the views of Aristotle fall short of the requirements of modern times, the 'Politics' will always form a valuable study for one who is likely to take part in the public affairs of his country.

CHAPTER VII.

THE NATURAL PHILOSOPHY OF ARISTOTLE.

ARISTOTLE has now done with Practical and Constructive Science.* He turns from Man with his disputations, reasonings, oratory, poetry, moral and social life, to the subjects of Speculative Science,—to Nature, the Universe, and God. In glancing at the series of great treatises in which the results of his thoughts and researches upon these subjects are embodied, it will be convenient to divide them under the three heads of Natural Philosophy, Biology, and Metaphysics. First, then, the 'Physical Discourse,' the treatise 'On the Heavens,' that 'On Generation and Destruction,' and the 'Meteorologics,' form together a distinct whole,† and contain the Natural Philosophy of Aristotle, of which let us now notice some of the salient points, leaving his Biology and Metaphysics to form the subject of future chapters.

Natural Philosophy, as conceived by Aristotle, was far more metaphysical than the science which is called by that name in the present day—a science based on

* See above, p. 42.
† On the connection of these works see some general remarks above, pp. 45, 46.

mathematics, and starting, we might perhaps say, with the doctrines of Newton's 'Principia,' anything which lies beyond these doctrines being taken for granted. But in Aristotle's Natural Philosophy nothing is taken for granted. He commences by inquiring into the nature of "Existence;" and sets himself to answer some of the puzzles with which his predecessors, the philosophers of Greece, had racked their own and other people's brains. They had said, "How is it possible for anything to come into existence? Out of what can it come? It must come either out of the existent or the non-existent. But it cannot come out of the existent, else it would have existed already; nor can it come out of the non-existent, for out of nothing nothing can come." Aristotle solves this dilemma ('Phys.' I. viii.) by introducing what now seems a simple enough distinction—that between the "possible" and the "actual;" things come into existence, that is, into actuality, out of the state of the possible. Now the possible, or potential, is in one sense non-existent, as it is nothing actual; but, on the other hand, it is not mere nonentity, as it is by hypothesis a possibility of existence. All this may appear to be a mere matter of words; and it may be asked what we gain by having the words "possibility" and "actuality" added to our vocabulary? But, in fact, men think by means of words; and if a new formula can clear up the notions connected with such often-occurring terms as "is" or "became," it is a gain, the reality of which is shown by the perplexities to which thinkers had been reduced to for the want of it.

Aristotle, pursuing his general reflections about Existence, says that in everything that exists you can trace three principles: the Matter out of which the thing arose, and which contained the possibility of its existence; the Form or actual nature which the thing possesses; and the Negation or Privation of all other natures. That is to say—a thing is what it is by not being what it is not. And thus all existence has a negative, as well as a positive, side ('Phys.' I. ix.) These remarks form a metaphysical basis to Natural Philosophy.

In the second book of his 'Physical Discourse,' Aristotle quits the region of pure abstractions, and states, in interesting terms, his views of "Nature." He speaks of "Nature" as "a principle of motion and rest essentially inherent in things, whether that motion be locomotion, increase, decay, or alteration." "It is absurd to try to prove the existence of Nature; its existence is self-evident." "Nature may be said in one way to be the simplest substratum of matter in things possessing their own principle of motion and change; in another way it may be called the form or law of such things." In other words, Nature is both matter or potentiality, and form or actuality; both the simple elements of a thing and its existence in perfection. It is also the transition from the one to the other. "Nature," says Aristotle, "spoken of as the creation of anything, is the path to nature."

Paley's 'Natural Theology' opens with the celebrated argument which compares the world to a watch. "If one were to find a watch," says Paley, "he would surely conclude that there must have been a watchmaker; and so from the marks of design in creation, which are like the adaptations to special purposes of each part in the watch, we must conclude that an intelligent Creator made the world." Aristotle, quite as strongly as Paley, admits the marks of design in nature. He says ('Phys.' II. viii. 14.): "The adaptation of means to ends which we see in the procedure of the animals makes some men doubt whether the spider, for instance, and the ant, do not work by the light of reason or an analogous faculty. In plants, moreover, manifest traces of a fit and wisely planned organisation appear. The swallow makes its nest and the spider its web by nature, and yet with a design and an end; and the roots of the plant grow downward for the sake of providing it with nourishment in the best way. It is plain, then, that the origin of natural things must be attributed to design." He repudiates the notion that "the heavens and the divinest of visible things" ('Phys.' II. iv. 6) can have been the result of the workings of blind chance. Nor will he accept the theory of Empedocles (which was like the Darwinian theory of Natural Selection in its extremest form) that blind chance hit upon the production of life, and that whole races of monsters and imperfect beings perished before the moment came when—by mere accident and coincidence—a creature was attained sufficiently perfect to survive ('Phys.' II. viii. 4). So far from chance having been the chief force in producing the framework of the Universe, Aristotle considers chance to be a mere exception, a mere irregularity, thwarting the reason and the wisdom which guides, and has ever guided, the operations of nature.

But, while utterly denying what Mr Darwin would seem to point to—that Reason is a result of the functions of matter, and is a comparatively recent development in the history of this globe—Aristotle would equally deny the thesis of Paley, that Reason, in the form of an intelligent Creator, existed separately before this world, and constructed the world as a watchmaker constructs a watch. While he considered Reason to have existed from all eternity, he thought that the Universe, pervaded in all its parts by Reason, had also existed from all eternity. Thus all idea of the world having been created was quite eliminated from the thoughts of Aristotle. He said the world *must* have been eternal, for everything which is created, or comes into existence, comes into the "actual" out of the "possible." The egg and the seed are instances of the "possible," the fowl and the flower of the "actual." But there must always have been a fowl before there was an egg, and a flower before there was a seed. Therefore the actual must always have been first; and if this be the case with particular classes of things, we cannot conceive that the whole world was ever non-existent, and a mere possibility waiting to be called into existence ('Metaphys.' VIII. viii.)

Philosophers always acknowledge the difficulty which there is in conceiving a *beginning*. Aristotle escapes this difficulty by asserting that the Universe has existed eternally the same as it appears to us now. He says that there is only one Cosmos or Universe, and that outside of this there is "neither space, nor vacuum, nor time." One would expect these words to mean that the Universe extends to infinity in all directions; but, on the other hand, Aristotle attributes a definite circular shape to the "outside" of the Universe, which would be incompatible with the idea of infinite extension. In fact, his arguments to prove the above untenable position are curious abstract quibbles, which may be quoted to show how oddly a philosopher of the 4th century B.C. could reason on the physical construction of the Universe. He says ('On the Heavens,' I. ix.) that there can be neither space nor vacuum outside the circumference of the Cosmos, for, if there were, then body might be placed therein; but this is impossible, because every physical body is naturally endowed with one of three motions: it is either naturally centripetal, or naturally centrifugal, or naturally revolving round the earth. Now each of these three kinds of body has its natural place within the Universe; the stone being centripetal has its natural place on or in the earth; fire being centrifugal has its natural place above the air; the stars which revolve have their natural place in the revolving Heaven. Thus there is no kind of body which can naturally exist outside the Universe, and therefore there can be no Space, for Space is that in which bodies exist! That there is no Time beyond the limits of the Universe, Aristotle proves by the more legitimate argument that "if there is no motion there can be no time, since Time is the measure of motion." But his conception of the "natural" motions inherent in different classes of bodies, and his appeal to his own preconceived ideas of "nature" to prove what exists, or does not exist, outside the circumference of Heaven, are very characteristic.

Time and Space, then, according to Aristotle, end with the circumference of Heaven, though it is difficult to understand how space can be conceived to come to an end at any particular point. But the Stagirite here becomes mystical, for he says that, "the things outside," existing in neither space nor time, enjoy for all eternity a perfect life of absolute joy and peace ('Heavens,' I. ix.) This is the region of the divine, in which there is life and consciousness, though perhaps no personality; it is increate, immutable, and indestructible.

Descending from this region—if that can be called *region* which is out of space altogether—we come in the Aristotelian system to the "First Heaven," the place of the fixed stars, which ever revolves with great velocity from the left to the right. In a lower sphere, revolving in the contrary direction, are the sun, moon, and planets; and we are told that we must not suppose that either stars or planets are composed of fire. Their substance is ether, that fifth element, or *quinta essentia*, which enters also into the composition of the human soul. They only seem bright, like fire, because the friction caused by the rapidity with which they are carried round makes them red-hot. The reason why the stars twinkle, but the planets do not, is merely that the former are so far off that our sight reaches them in a weak and trembling condition; hence their light seems to us to quiver, while really it is our eyesight which is quivering. Sun, moon, and stars alike are living beings, unwearied, and in the enjoyment of perfect happiness.

It has often been said that if an ancient Greek temple be compared with a Gothic cathedral, the one suggests the idea of the finite, the other of the infinite. The same thing might be said of Aristotle's Cosmology when compared with the views of modern science. Aristotle figured to himself a perfectly limited universe, with the earth in the centre, and the fixed stars all round the circumference. In a circle, or globe, it may be questioned which is the place of honour—the centre or the circumference. The Pythagoreans, accordingly, after the abstract method of those times, declared that the centre must be the most honourable position, and that, as the element fire is more honourable than the element earth, the centre of the Universe must be occupied by some Central Fire, and that the earth must revolve round this like the other stars. Aristotle, unconscious how much nearer to the truth this guess was than his own, laughs at it as the production of men "who try to square facts to their own fancies, and who wish to have a share in the arrangement of the Universe." He also repudiates ('Heavens,' II. xiv. 1) the theory of Plato that the earth is packed round the axis of the entire Universe and revolves with it, thus causing day and night.* He maintains that the earth is the motionless

* There is some doubt as to what Plato's theory actually was. See 'Minor Works of George Grote,' vol. i. pp. 239-275, and Professor Jowett's Introduction to the 'Timæus' of Plato.

centre, but the least honourable member, of the Universe, the all-embracing circumference being the most noble, and the heavenly bodies having a dignity in inverse ratio to their approach towards the centre. The guesses, or intuitions, of the ancient Greeks in Aristotle's time, or soon afterwards, hit upon something very like an anticipation of the Copernican system. And this was especially the case with Aristarchus of Samos, who announced the double movement of the earth, round its own axis and round the sun. But Aristotle certainly contributed nothing towards the adoption of such ideas. He unfortunately committed himself, on fancied grounds of symmetry, to an opposite view.

Aristotle argued that if the earth were to move it could only do so "unnaturally," by the application of external force in contradiction to its own natural tendency to rest round the centre, and that no such forced movement could be kept up for ever, whereas the arrangements of the Cosmos must be for all eternity. Therefore the earth must be at rest! As to its shape, Aristotle was more correct: he proved it to be spherical —(1) by the consideration that all heavy bodies are by nature always tending to the centre, and that this process must result in the production of a spherical mass; (2) by the fact that the earth's shadow cast on the moon in an eclipse is circular. He considered the bulk of the earth to be small when compared with that of "the other stars;" he accepts the calculations of the geometers of his time that its circumference was 400,000 stades; and he says that "we must not treat with incredulity the opinion of those who say that the regions near the Pillars of Hercules (or Straits of Gibraltar) join on to India, and that the ocean to the east of India and that to the west of Europe are one and the same." In support of this proposition he adduces the fact that elephants are to be found on each side, *i.e.*, in India and in Africa ('Heavens,' II. xiv. 15). The passage of Aristotle here quoted had a large share in inflaming the imagination of Christopher Columbus, and in sending him forth from the coasts of Spain in search of the coasts of India; and it was the cause of the islands of Central America being named the "West Indies," and the *aborigines* of North America being called "Red Indians." As an approximative guess at the size and figure of the earth, the passage in question was not a bad one, considering the time when it was written; but curiously enough it contains two errors, the first of which would imply the earth to be a great deal larger, and the second a great deal smaller, than it really is. The mean geographical stade of the Greeks is computed at 168 yards 1 foot and 6 inches, and thus if 400,000 stades be assigned to the circumference of the earth, we get a measurement of above 38,000 miles, whereas the latest calculations would only give about 24,857 miles for a mean circumference of the earth. Thus evidently the geometers of the time of Aristotle were too liberal in their ideas of the earth's size. But, on the other hand, those who identified the Atlantic with the Pacific Ocean, and brought India opposite to Spain, had evidently too contracted a notion of the contents of our globe.

Owing to the absence of astronomical instruments,

and the generally infantile condition of physical science in the 4th century B.C., it was only natural that the *a priori* method, or *guessing*, should greatly predominate in the cosmical theories of that time. But Aristotle's strength did not lie in his imagination. In this faculty he was inferior to other philosophers whom in analytical power he far surpassed. Thus Alexander von Humboldt says of him ('Cosmos,' vol. i. note 48), "the great influence which the writings of Aristotle exercised on the whole of the Middle Ages, renders it a cause of extreme regret that he should have been so opposed to the grander and juster views of the fabric of the universe entertained by the more ancient Pythagorean school." There was, in fact, a want of sublimity in the fancy of Aristotle, and it so happened that he sometimes contemptuously rejected hypotheses which were not only more beautiful, but more true, than his own. We have seen that this was the case with regard to the earth's position in the cosmical system. And the same thing occurred as to the nature of comets. The Pythagoreans had declared comets to be "planets of long revolution;" but Aristotle, rejecting this supposition, affirmed them to be transient meteors of our atmosphere, formed out of luminous or incandescent matter which had been thrown off by the stars. And to explain the reason why comets are so rare, he said that the matter out of which they are composed is constantly used up in forming the Milky Way. ('Meteorol.' I. viii.) "The nebulous belt, then, which traverses the vault of the heavens, is regarded by the

Stagirite as an immense comet incessantly reproducing itself."

Clearly, Aristotle's contribution to Natural Philosophy did not consist in suggesting or leading the way to true views as to the nature and arrangement of the heavenly bodies. He not only was not in advance of his age in this respect, but was even behind it, in so far as he refused to adopt theories, which have since turned out to have been anticipations of the results of modern science. But, on the other hand, it must be remembered that those theories were incapable of verification at the time, and had no force in themselves to command the attention of the world. They were like the "false dawn" in tropical countries, which appears for a few minutes and then fades way, allowing the darkness again to reign supreme, till the true sunrise takes place. Unconvinced by the speculations of the Pythagorean school and of Aristarchus of Samos, the great Alexandrian astronomer, Ptolemy, in the second century of our era, reaffirmed the Aristotelian views as to the spherical form and motion of the heavens, as to the earth's position in the centre of the heavens, and as to its being devoid of any motion of translation. And the Ptolemaic system satisfied men's minds until, with Copernicus and Galileo, modern astronomy began.

We must allow that Aristotle's cosmical ideas were erroneous and misleading. Still we must take them as constituting a mere fraction of his encyclopædia of philosophy, and we must recollect that they are put forth in works which laid out and constituted new sciences.

This was the Stagirite's achievement,—the clear analytic separation of the different sciences, and the statement, in outline at all events, of the questions which each science had to answer. Aristotle generally attempted to furnish his own answer to these questions, and often gave wrong answers; yet to have posited the questions at all was a great matter, and cleared the way for the thoughts of subsequent generations. There is no one to whose work the saying is more appropriate than to that of the Stagirite—*prudens quæstio dimidium scientiæ est*—" It is half-way to knowledge when you know what you have to inquire."

The leading questions started in the Natural Philosophy of Aristotle are as to the nature of causation, time, space, and motion. On the subject of motion he went astray by taking up the idea that celestial and terrestrial motions were different in kind—that the heavenly bodies "naturally" revolved, while bodies on earth had each a natural motion in them, either downward or upward. This belief in the absolute levity of certain bodies—as, for instance, fire—was, of course, a mistake. "Truth is the daughter of Time;" and a few of the great discoveries of modern ages, which appear so simple, though they were so hardly and so late achieved,—such as the Copernican system, and the law of gravitation,—have shattered the Cosmos of Aristotle. Still it required at least fifteen centuries before anything like a demonstration was brought against the reality of that Cosmos and its arrangements. Thus, if Aristotle be censured for the incorrectness of his theories, succeeding generations of thinkers for so long a period must also be held responsible for their undoubting acceptance of them.

Aristotle's method in Physics, as in most other subjects, consisted in this: he first endeavoured to state clearly to himself what was the problem which he had before him, then he collected all the solutions of that problem which had been proposed by his predecessors, and all popular "sayings" and "notions" in regard to it, and then he examined existing opinions by the light of such facts as occurred to him, or which had been previously collected by him, or else he applied logical reasonings and general philosophical considerations in pronouncing upon the validity of the theories of others. A main part of the process consisted in starting ingenious difficulties to the theories in question, so that they seldom came through the ordeal without being wholly exploded or considerably modified. The residuum left, or the new result arrived at, constituted the theory of Aristotle. Such is not the procedure by which discoveries are made, knowledge increased, and the boundaries of science extended, in modern times. But after all, it was not a bad procedure for a man who was writing an encyclopædia. Aristotle had undertaken to set forth every department of knowledge revised and perfected, so far as possible, by the aid of stores of information and thought which he had laid up. In some departments he was much stronger than others: in Politics, Sociology, Psychology, and Natural History, he had a far better array of facts than in Astronomy and Mechanics. No one could be keener than he was to make facts the basis of every theory; but he was obliged to do the best he could in each case with his materials. He set out all that was known or believed on each subject, and added to the knowledge or criticised the beliefs as well as he could. The real aids for the advance and verification of science which exist in modern times—instruments, such as the telescope, the microscope, the barometer, the thermometer, the spectroscope, and countless others; the knowledge of many great laws of nature; and the practice of accurately observing and carefully recording,—were all wanting in the days of Aristotle. Therefore it is absurd to treat him as if he had been a modern man of science, with a vicious method. It may be called a mistake that he attempted so much; still what he accomplished was wonderful if we merely regard it as a map of the Sciences belonging to the 4th century B.C., full of his own additions and improvements.

There is one great science of modern days which Aristotle failed to separate off, or sketch out, or in any way to foreshadow—and that is the science of Chemistry. Some erroneously spell this word "chymistry" as though it were derived from the Greek *chymos*,* a juice, and as though it had been known to the Greeks. But of course "chemistry" comes from the Semitic word *chem* (which is the same as "Ham," the son of Noah), meaning "black," and then "Egyptian." And thus

---

* Aristotle, in treating of the sense of Taste, gives an enumeration of different flavours, and then says, "The other properties of juices form a proper subject for inquiry in connection with the physiology of plants." Thus by "juices" he means vegetable fluids, to be treated of from the point of view of Botany or of *Materia Medica*.

Chemistry is the black or Egyptian art, having taken its rise out of the searches made by the Alchemists to discover the philosopher's stone. Aristotle had no notion whatever of the rich field of knowledge and power which lay in the analysis of substances. He had no idea of the composition of water or air. The crucible and the retort had never been worked in Athens; the most superficial guess-work, as to what we should call the chemical properties of bodies, contented the philosophers of the day. Aristotle's work 'On Generation and Corruption' would have been the appropriate place for enunciating some of the laws of Chemistry; but he does not go beyond a resolution of the "Four Elements" into the ultimate principles of the Hot, the Cold, the Wet, and the Dry — the first pair being "active" and the second "passive" principles. Hot and Wet, we are told, form Air; Hot and Dry, Fire; Cold and Wet, Water; Cold and Dry, Earth. From these principles Aristotle deduces the generation and destruction of physical bodies; but on the details of a theory which now seems puerile we need not dwell.

CHAPTER VIII.

THE BIOLOGY OF ARISTOTLE.

THE word "Biology" is perhaps only about fifty years old, having first come into prominent use in the 'Positive Philosophy' of Auguste Comte. It is now quite naturalised in the vocabulary of science; and there is an article on "Biology," by Professor Huxley, in the recently published edition of the 'Encyclopædia Britannica,' which begins, "The Biological sciences are those which deal with the phenomena manifested by living matter." Yet still, in the eyes of a scholar this modern compound is an unfortunate one. The Greeks had two words for life, *Zöé* and *Bios:* the former expressed life viewed from the inside, as it were—the vital principle, the functions of life, the sense of living; the latter expressed the external form and manner of living, such as a man's profession or career. *Zöé* was applicable to the whole animated kingdom; *Bios* was restricted to man, except so far as, half-metaphorically, it was applied to the habits of beasts or birds. Thus Aristotle divided *Zöé* into the species "vegetable," "animal," and "human;" but *Bios* into the species "life of pleasure," "life of ambition," and "life of thought." From all this, it will be seen that "Biology" could not be used to denote a science of the phenomena of living matter in general, without a sacrifice of ancient Greek associations. "Biology," in short, is more appropriate to express what we generally call Sociology; and, on the other hand, "Zoölogy" should have been used to express what is now called "Biology." But the fact was, that the word "Zoölogy" (derived from *Zöon*, an animal, not from *Zöé*, life) had been already appropriated as a name for natural history. Hence, without regard to classical propriety, the word "Biology" was forced into service to meet a want, and to express, what had never been expressed before, the science of life in all its manifestations from the lowest ascidian up to the highest development of humanity, so far as that development can be considered to be a natural evolution out of the physiological laws of life.

Aristotle had no word to express this comprehensive idea, but assuredly he had the idea itself. He regards the whole of nature as a continuous chain, even beginning with inorganic substances and passing by imperceptible gradations on to organisms, to the vegetable, and to the zoophyte, and then to the animal and the various ranks in the animal kingdom, and lastly to man ('Researches about Animals,' VIII. i. 4), "whose soul in childhood, you might say, differs not from the soul of the lower animals." This broad comprehensive sweep of the philosophic eye through the realms of nature, this finding of unity in such endless diversity, this tracing of a continuous thread throughout the ascending scale of life, may seem quite a matter of course to educated persons of the present day. But it was creditable to Aristotle to have so fully arrived at and entertained this conception, and to have set it forth in such firmly-drawn scientific outlines. Above all, it was creditable to one who, though born of the race of Esculapius (see above, p. 3), had been trained as a dialectician and an orator, and had devoted so much time and labour to the sciences connected with words and thoughts, that he should have had the force and versatility to act also as pioneer into a totally different range of inquiries, and to collect such a mass of facts wherewith to fill in his general sketch of animated nature. It is probable that at all periods of his life his studies, observations, and notes upon matters of physical and natural science, ran on side by side with his development of mental and moral philosophy. Some have thought that the period of his residence at the Court of Macedonia, when acting as tutor to Alexander, afforded him peculiar facilities, in the shape of royal menageries and hunters and fowlers under his command, for the collection of materials for his great work on animals. However this may be, there seems no sufficient reason for taking that work itself out of the list of those which were on the stocks and more or less completed during the last thirteen years of his life.

Aristotle's biological treatises, as briefly specified above (p. 47), consist (1) of the work 'On the Parts of Animals,' which contains a distinction still valid in physiology between "tissues" and "organs," or as Aristotle calls them, "homogeneous" and "unhomogeneous" substances. He traces here, according to his own ideas, the ascent from the inorganic to the organic world: out of heat, cold, wetness, and dryness the four elements are compounded; out of the four elements are formed the homogeneous substances or tissues; out of these are formed the organs, and out of the organs the organised being. All this served as a provisional theory, until superseded by the discoveries of chemistry. Aristotle laid it down as a principle of method ('Parts of An.,' I. i. 4), that all which was common to the various species of living beings should be discussed before entering upon their specific differences. Therefore (2) the treatise 'On the Soul' followed next in order, and traced out the vital principle through its successive ascending manifestations. To this was appended (3) the 'Parva Naturalia' or 'Physiological Tracts,' which dealt with some of the functions of living creatures, whether common or special, such as sensation, memory, dreaming, and also with the following pairs of opposites: waking and sleeping, youth and old age, inspiration and expiration, life and death. It was added that there is another pair still to be treated of—namely, health and sickness. The Stagirite, as was natural from his family traditions, always appears to have looked forward to composing a philosophical work on Medicine. But there is no trace of this ever having been achieved.

The 4th book on the list kept still to generalities. This was the short treatise 'On the Locomotion of Animals,' which showed how various organs in the various creatures are adapted by nature for this purpose. Next (5) the elaborate treatise 'On the Generation of Animals' worked out this subject, illustrating it with a wonderfully copious collection of facts, or supposed facts, and of the opinions of the day; and, lastly (6), the great treatise entitled 'Researches about Animals,' formed, as it were, the conclusion of the whole, by giving detailed observations upon many of the various living creatures which are the products of the working of nature's general laws.

Aristotle justly drew a distinction between the way in which any phenomenon of nature would be considered and defined by a dialectician and by a physicist. Thus he says ('On the Soul,' I. i. 16): "Anger would be defined by a dialectician to be 'a desire for retaliation,' or something of the kind,—by a physical philosopher it would be defined as 'a boiling up of the hot blood about the heart.'" It is needless to say that the Stagirite himself was great and unrivalled in his dialectical definitions,—those definitions which depended on grasping the essence of facts which are patent to all ages alike; while in his physical definitions, being destitute of facts which only later ages have brought to light, he was very imperfect and occasionally almost absurd. As a specimen of this we may mention his account of the vital principle or life, from the two points of view. He defines the vital principle ('Soul,' II. i. 6) to be "the essential actuality of an organism;" and this definition has met with high praise from modern physiologists, some of whom, indeed, appear simply to have repeated it in slightly different words. Thus Duges defines life as "the special activity of organised bodies;" and Beclard calls it "organisation in action."* The merit of Aristotle's definition, as coming from an ancient Greek philosopher, consists in its avoiding the view which would have been natural in those times—namely, that life, the vital principle or the physical soul, was a separate entity, dwelling in the body, *hospes comesque corporis*, "the body's guest and friend," as the Emperor Hadrian called it in his dying verses. Aristotle said that life, or the soul, is not a chance guest, but a function; it is to the body as sight is to the eye; it is the perfect action of all the conditions of the bodily organisation. Thus the Pythagoreans spoke vainly when they talked of the "transmigration of souls," as if the soul of a man could migrate into the body of a beast. "You might as well," said Aristotle, "speak of the carpenter's art (which is the result of the carpenter's tools) migrating into flutes, which are the tools of the musician."

So much for his dialectical, or speculative, views of life. The following are some of his opinions in detail on the same subject, from a physical point of view, taken from the 'Physiological Tracts:'—The primary condition of life is the "natural fire" which resides in the heart of each living creature. This fire may be extinguished by contrary forces, or smothered by excess of heat. Respiration is the process of cooling, which prevents the smothering of the vital fire. Animals require two things for existence—food and

* These definitions are quoted in Bennett's 'Text-book of Physiology,' p. 184. See also Mr G. H. Lewes's 'Aristotle, a Page from the History of Science,' p. 230.

cooling. The mouth serves for both purposes, except in the case of fishes,* who get their cooling not by air through the lungs, but by water through the gills. The heart is placed in the middle region of the body, and is not only the seat of life, but also of intelligence; it is the first formed of all the parts. The brain is the coldest and wettest part of the body, and serves conjointly with the respiration in cooling down the fire of life. Three of the senses—sight, sound, and smell—are located in the brain; touch and taste reside in the heart, which also contains the "common sensorium," or faculty of complex perceptions, such as figure, size, motion, and number. The heart makes the blood and sends it out by the "veins" to all parts of the body (of course Aristotle was unaware of the return of the blood to the heart, and therefore made no distinction between veins and arteries). Adequate warmth being the condition of life, the inhabitants of hot countries are longer-lived than those of cold countries; and men are longer-lived than women. But as cooling also is required, people with large heads, as a rule, live long.

It is hardly necessary to say that every opinion above mentioned is mistaken, and almost every statement of fact erroneous. Aristotle, however, is not solely responsible for the doctrines, for he doubtless inherited his ideas of anatomy and physiology from Hippocrates and his father Nicomachus, and, in short,

* Aristotle rejects the (true) opinion of Anaxagoras and Diogenes that fishes get air out of the water which they draw through their gills, and that they are suffocated when out of the water because the air comes to them in too large quantities.

from his Greek predecessors. He neither did, nor could, create the whole of physiology afresh, as he created the whole science of logic. This shows the difference between a science that is simple and abstract, being dependent on a few laws of the human mind, and a science which is infinitely complex, being dependent on facts which have only gradually been discovered up to a certain point during the long lapse of centuries, with the aid of instruments which were unknown to the ancients. But Aristotle had distinctly the idea of the advance of physiology and medicine by means of the study of nature. He said, "Physical philosophy leads to medical deductions, the best doctors seek grounds for their art in nature." Perhaps from this sentence, at all events from the notion contained in it, the word "physician" has come to be appropriated in modern times by the practitioners of medicine.

Unfortunately, Aristotle not unfrequently applied dialectical reasonings to questions of physiology when they were quite inappropriate. For instance, arguing against Plato's theory of respiration — namely, that breathing results from the impact upon us of the external atmosphere following upon the disturbance which is caused by the expiration of warm air—he says that this would imply expiration to be the first of the two operations; but they alternate, and expiration is the last, *therefore* inspiration must be the first! Again, he mentions the opinion of those who said that the senses correspond with the four elements, and that sight is fire, trying to prove it by the fact that if the eye be struck sparks are seen. Aristotle, however, says that this fact is to be explained in another way: the iris of the eye shines like a phosphorescent substance; when the eye is struck, the sudden shock of the blow causes the eye as an object of vision to become separate from the eye as the organ of vision, and thus the eye for an instant sees itself! Again, he says that the "white" of the eye is unctuous, which prevents the watery vehicle that conveys the sight from getting frozen; the eye is less liable to freeze than any part of the body!

Turning from these curiosities of an old-world physiology, let us glance at the natural history of Aristotle. There is something peculiar and Aristotelian about the very terms "Natural History." They arise out of a mistranslation of the title of Aristotle's work, 'Histories about Animals,' where "Histories" is used in its primitive sense of "investigations" or "researches." But the title has been translated *Historia Animalium*, or 'History of Animals,' and from this the modern phrase "Natural History" has doubtless got crystallised into its present signification. Looking to the contents of the treatise in question, we perceive that to a great part of it the shorter form of the word "Histories" would have been applicable, as consisting rather of "Stories about Animals" than of any very profound investigations with regard to them. It is probable that a large proportion of what is here recorded came to Aristotle orally; and that, too, not from *savants*, but from uneducated classes of people whose occupations had put them in the way of observing the habits of certain species — such people as fishermen, sailors, sponge-divers, fowlers, hunters, herdsmen, bee-keepers, and the like. We know how difficult it is to get pure fact, unalloyed by fancy, from informants of this kind; and therefore it is no wonder that Aristotle, in compiling the first treatise on Natural History that was ever written, and in collecting his materials by inquiry made at first or second hand from the working classes, should have admitted many a "yarn" and many a "traveller's tale" into his pages. The subject was too new to admit of his being able by instinctive sagacity to reject the improbable; a judgment of that kind is only attained by one who possesses a vast stock of well-ascertained facts, and by unconscious analogy can argue from the known to the unknown. In many cases Aristotle shows himself almost as simple as old Herodotus, with his tales of the phœnix and other marvels.

The following may be quoted as one instance out of many of the *naïveté* of the Stagirite ('Animals,' IX. xlviii.): "Among marine animals there are many instances recorded of the mild, gentle disposition of the dolphin, and of its love of its children, and its affection, in the neighbourhood of Tarentum, Caria, and other places. It is said that when a dolphin was captured and wounded on the coast of Caria, a great multitude of dolphins came into the harbour, until the fisherman let him go, when they all went away together. And one large dolphin always follows the little ones to take care of them. And sometimes a shoal of large and small dolphins has been seen together, and two of these having been left behind have appeared soon after supporting and carrying on their back a small dead dolphin that was on the point of sinking, as if in pity for it, that it might not be devoured by any other creature. Incredible things are told of the swiftness of the dolphin, which appears to be the swiftest of all animals whether marine or terrestrial. They even leap over the masts of large ships. This is especially the case when they pursue a fish for the sake of food; for if it flies from them they will pursue it, from hunger, into the depths of the sea. And when they have to return from a great depth, they hold in their breath, as if calculating the distance, and gathering themselves up they shoot forward like an arrow, wishing with all speed to accomplish the distance to their breathing-place. And if a ship happen to be in the way, they will leap over its masts. The males and females live in pairs with each other. There is some doubt why they cast themselves on shore, for it is said that they do this at times without any apparent reason."

The freshness of spirit which breathes through this passage characterises the whole of Aristotle's treatise, which, in spite of its sometimes reminding us of the "showman" of modern times, has excited the enthusiastic admiration of several great authorities. Cuvier says, "I cannot read this work without being ravished with astonishment. Indeed it is impossible to conceive how a single man was able to collect and compare the multitude of particular facts implied in the numerous rules and aphorisms which are contained in this book." Buffon, De Blainville, St Hilaire, and others,* have used similar terms of eulogy. One modern zoologist, Professor Sundevall of Stockholm, has reckoned up the number of species with which Aristotle showed himself to be more or less acquainted, and he finds them to amount to nearly 500,—the total number of mammals described or indicated being about 70; of birds 150; of reptiles 20; and of fishes 116—making altogether 356 species of vertebrate animals. Of the invertebrate classes about 60 species of insects and arachnids seem to have been known to Aristotle; some 24 crustaceans and annelids; and about 40 molluscs and radiates.† At the same time, it must be remembered that Aristotle had no idea of the scientific system of classification which appears in Professor Sundevall's list. He does not seem to have laboured much at the arrangement of living creatures into natural orders; indeed he could not have succeeded in such an attempt, for want of a sufficient knowledge of anatomy. He was content with the superficial, universally-received, grouping of animals, as walking, creeping, flying, or swimming; as oviparous or viviparous; aquatic or terrestrial; and the like. His book contains a mass of materials, but without much methodic arrangement or trace of system. It pointed the way, however, for his successors to a science of zoology.

The facts given by him of course vary extremely in correctness and in value. In his account of sponges,

* Quoted by Mr G. H. Lewes in his 'Aristotle,' p. 270.
† See 'The Natural History Review' for 1864, p. 494.

for instance, Aristotle is thought to have shown sound information, probably derived from the reports of the professional divers. But his statements about bees, though obtained, as he tells us, from bee-keepers, and though "made beautiful for ever" in the charming verses of Virgil's fourth Georgic, have been quite overturned by the microscopic discoveries of Reaumur, Hunter, Huber, Keys, Vicat, and Dunbar. On one cardinal point the ancients were all wrong: they did not understand the sex and the functions of either the queen-bee, the worker, or the drone.

The following account of the lion is considered to be fairly correct ('An.,' IX. xliv.): "When feeding, the lion is extremely savage; but when he is not hungry and is full fed, he is quite gentle. He is not either jealous or suspicious. He is playful and affectionate towards those animals which have been brought up with him, and to which he is accustomed. When hunted, so long as he is in view he never flies or cowers; and if compelled to give way by the number of his hunters, he retreats leisurely, at a walk, turning himself round at short intervals. But if he reaches a covert he flies rapidly, until he is in the open again, and then he again retreats at a walk. If compelled to fly when on the open plains, he runs at full stretch, but does not leap. His manner of running is continuous, like that of a dog at full stretch; when pursuing his prey, however, he throws himself upon it when he comes within reach. It is true what they say about the lion being very much afraid of fire (as Homer wrote, 'the blazing fagots, that his courage daunt'), and about his watching and singling out for attack the person who has struck him. But when any one misses hitting him and only annoys him, if in his rush he succeeds in catching that person, he does not harm him nor wound him with his claws, but shakes and frightens him and then leaves him. Lions are more disposed to enter towns and attack mankind when they have grown old, because old age renders them unable to hunt, and because of the decay of their teeth. They live many years; and in the case of a lame lion who was captured, he had many of his teeth worn down, which some considered a sign that lions live long, for this could not have happened to an animal who was not aged."

The 'Researches about Animals,' like many other of Aristotle's great treatises, appears to have been left in an unfinished state. The tenth book seems merely to be a sort of fragmentary continuation of the seventh book—both treating of the reproduction of the human species. In the ten books as they have come down to us, no one can pretend to find a finished whole. It is a question, therefore, whether the work was ever published in Aristotle's lifetime, or whether it ever got, in its present form, to the Alexandrian Library. In the Alexandrian Catalogue, indeed, there is mention of a work entitled 'Animals' in nine books. But this may have been a set of excerpts by some Peripatetic scholar; we cannot tell what its exact relation to "*Our* Aristotle" may have been. There is some little interest in the question, on account of the influence that Aristotle is supposed to have exercised on the Septuagint version of the Old Testament, which was begun at Alexandria 285 B.C.—that is to say, just after Aristotle's

MSS had been carried off to Asia Minor. It has been conjectured that the Septuagint translators, in rendering the Hebrew word *arnebeth*, or "hare," by the Greek word *dasypus* (hairy-foot), instead of by the word *lagos*, which had been usual in earlier classical Greek, were following a new fashion set by Aristotle in his 'Researches about Animals,' in which work "the modern word *dasypus* had almost entirely superseded the older."* And it is added that "there was an even yet more striking example of Aristotle's influence on the passage" (Leviticus, xi. 6): for whereas in the original Hebrew text the hare was said to chew the cud, the translators, having been enlightened by the natural history of Aristotle, "boldly interpolated the word NOT into the sacred text." The facts of the case are—that Aristotle uses *lagos* for "hare" indifferently with, and nearly as often as, *dasypus*; and that in one passage ('An.,' III. xxi. 1) he cursorily contrasts the hare with the class of ruminants. On the whole, then, it seems most natural to believe that the Septuagint translators used the word *dasypus* because it had become the fashion in speaking Greek to use it, and that Aristotle himself had obeyed and not created this fashion. With regard to the other point, it is quite possible that the translators may have seen that passage of Aristotle's above referred to; at all events, as educated men, they were doubtless influenced by the spread of the study of natural history, to which Aristotle, who had died only thirty-seven years before, had given great impetus.

* Dean Stanley's 'Lectures on the History of the Jewish Church,' iii. 261.

CHAPTER IX.

THE METAPHYSICS OF ARISTOTLE.

SOME of Aristotle's earliest attempts at writing were on a strictly metaphysical subject, when he attacked the Platonic doctrine of "Ideas." He doubtless went on from this beginning, and thought of metaphysical questions all his life, till he had framed for himself a more or less complete metaphysical system, traces of which show themselves in many forms of expression and leading thoughts in all his various scientific works. But it seems as if he had put off to the last the undertaking of a direct and complete exposition of that system; and hence arose the name "Metaphysics," which is a mere title signifying "the things which follow after physics"—a title given by Aristotle's school to a mass of papers which they edited after his death, and with regard to which they wished to indicate that chronologically these papers were composed *after* the physical treatises, and also, perhaps, that the subject of which they treated was *above* * and *beyond* the mere physical conditions of *things*. The word "Meta-

---

* Thus Shakespeare speaks of "Fate and *metaphysical* aid," meaning "supernatural."

physics," starting from this fortuitous origin, has come to be generally understood in modern times as denoting the most abstract of the sciences—the science of the forms of thought and the forms of things, the science of knowing and being, the science that answers the questions, How can we know anything? how can anything exist? Aristotle, who, of course, was himself unconscious of the word "Metaphysics," had three names which he used indifferently for this science. Sometimes he called it simply "Wisdom;" sometimes "First Philosophy," as treating of primary substances and the origin of things; sometimes "Theology," because all things have their root in the divine nature.

We have already had some specimens of Aristotle's metaphysical doctrines, put forward as a foundation for natural philosophy (see above, p. 132). In his biological treatises also, especially in that 'On the Soul,' Aristotle does not confine himself to the physical principle of life and the functions of the animal soul, but enters upon the mode of our acquiring knowledge, on perception, memory, reason, and the relation of the mind to external objects—all being questions which encroach upon the province of metaphysical inquiry. The substantive treatise, bearing the name 'Metaphysics,' has come down to us in the shape of a posthumous fragment, which has been edited and eked out by the addition of other papers. The whole work, as it stands, consists of thirteen books. Of these, seven books were written by Aristotle as the setting forth of his ontology, or science of existence; Books IX., XII., and XIII. (on the Pythagorean and Platonic systems of numbers and ideas) seem to have been intended to come in as part of the same treatise, but to have been left by Aristotle in the condition of mere notes or materials; Book XI. is thought to be a separate, though very valuable and interesting, essay on the nature of the Deity; while Books IV. and X., and the appendix to Book I., are un-Aristotelian,* and should never have had a place assigned to them in the 'Metaphysics.'

To turn to this work from the 'Researches about Animals' is like turning from White's 'Selborne' to Kant's 'Critic of the Pure Reason.' Metaphysical questions are necessarily abstruse, dry, and difficult; but the attempt has sometimes been made—as, for instance, by Plato, Berkeley, Hume, and Ferrier—to discuss them in clear, pointed language, as little as possible removed from the ordinary language of literature. Aristotle, on the other hand, at all events in later life, aimed only at scientific precision; and his 'Metaphysics' is the forerunner of those German philosophies which from beginning to end exhibit a jargon of technical phraseology. In another respect, also, Aristotle here sets an example which has been much followed by the Germans during the present century; for in Book I. he gives a "history of philosophy" from Thales down to himself. This is a very

---

* Book IV. consists of a list of philosophical terms and their definitions, perhaps jotted down by some scholar. Book X. is a paraphrase of part of the 'Physical Discourse.' The appendix to Book I. is a little essay on First Principles, of which tradition attributes the authorship to one Pasides.

interesting little sketch, disclosing for the first time the fact that human thought has a history, and that there was a time when the word "cause," for instance, had never been heard, and pointing to the conclusion that every abstract word which we use is the result of the theories, and perhaps the controversies, of former ages. Aristotle traces the thoughts of successive Grecian thinkers, advancing under a law, while each stage at which they arrived forced them on to the next (see 'Met.,' I., iii. 11), from about 600 B.C. to about 330 B.C. And this task had never been again so well accomplished until Hegel gave his first set of lectures on the History of Philosophy, at Jena, in 1805. Hegel was followed in the same field by Brandis, Schwegler, Ueberweg, Cousin, Renouvier, Ferrier, Zeller, and many others, to whose works we must refer for information as to the Greek philosophers. Suffice it to say, that Aristotle's method of procedure is to take his own doctrine of the Four Causes (see above, p. 72), and to show how at first philosophers only got hold of the idea of a Material Cause, and that afterwards they gradually arrived at the idea of Motive Power, Form, and End, or Final Cause. On the whole, his brief and masterly sketch, while full of points of light, is open to the charge of not doing sufficient justice to the views of his predecessors. Among them all, he seems most highly to appreciate Anaxagoras, of whom he says that, by introducing the idea of Reason among the causes of the existence of the world, he was "like a sober man beginning to speak amidst a party of drunkards." Aristotle repeats here his old polemic against what he calls the system of Plato, though it is doubtful whether Plato would himself have acknowledged it. One would almost say that Aristotle misstated Plato in order to refute him.

The same fate, as if by way of reprisal, has often in modern times befallen the Stagirite, who has repeatedly been misstated, and then censured for what he never had maintained. At the risk, however, of committing fresh injustices of this sort, we will endeavour briefly to sum up his views upon some of the greatest questions which have occupied modern philosophers. First, then, we may ask how would Aristotle have dealt with those problems concerning the existence of Matter, and the reality of the External World, which have been a "shibboleth" in the philosophic world from Bishop Berkeley, through the days of Hume and the Scotch psychologists, down to Kant and Hegel and the extreme idealists of Germany? His utterances on this subject are perhaps chiefly to be found in the third book of his treatise 'On the Soul,' beginning with the fourth chapter. On turning to them we see that he never separates existence from knowledge. "A thing in actual existence," he says, "is identical with the knowledge of that thing." Again—"The possible existence of a thing is identical with the possibility in us of perceiving or knowing it." Thus, until a thing is perceived or known, it can only be said to have a potential or possible existence. And from this a doctrine very similar to that of Ferrier might be deduced, that "nothing exists except *plus* me"—that is to say, in relation to some mind perceiving it. Aristotle indicates, without fully explaining, his doctrine of the relation of the mind to external things in a celebrated passage ('Soul,' iii. v.), where he says that there are two kinds of Reason in the soul—the one passive, the other constructive. "The passive Reason *becomes* all things by receiving their impress; the constructive Reason *creates* all things, just as light brings colours into actual existence, while without light they would have remained mere possibilities." Aristotle, then, appears to be removed from the "common-sense" doctrine of "natural realism," which believes that the world would be just what we perceive to be, even if there were no one to perceive it; for, by his analogy, the mind contributes as much to the existence of things as light does to colour; and he is equally removed from that extreme idealism which would represent things to be merely the thoughts of a mind, for he evidently considers that there is a "not-me"—a factor in all existence and knowledge—which is outside of the mind, and which may be taken to be symbolised by all the constituents of colour, except light: the mind, according to him, contributes only what light does to colour; all else is external to the mind, though without the mind nothing could attain to actuality. The external world, then, according to Aristotle, is a perfectly real existence, but it is the product of two sets of factors—the one being the rich and varied constituents of the universe, the other being Reason manifested in perceiving minds; and, without the presence and co-operation of this perceptive Reason, all things would be at once condemned to virtual annihilation.

As to Matter, Aristotle called it "timber," or "the underlying," to indicate that it is to existence as wood is to a table, and that it is something which is implied in all existence. Nothing can exist without Matter, which is one of the four causes of the existence of everything; but, on the other hand, it may be said that Matter itself has no existence. Things can only be realised by the mind, and so come into actual existence, if they be endowed with Form; pure Matter denuded of form cannot be perceived or known, and therefore cannot be actual. Suppose we take marble as the matter or material of which a statue is composed,— if we think of the marble we attribute to it qualities —colour, brilliancy, hardness, and so on, and these qualities constitute Form, and the marble is no longer pure Matter. We have to ask, then, what is the matter "underlying" the marble? and again, if we figure to ourselves anything possessing definite qualities—as, for instance, any of the simple substances of chemistry— we at once have not only matter, but form. Matter, thus, in the theory of Aristotle, is something which must always be presupposed, and which yet always eludes us, and flies back from the region of the actual into that of the possible. Ultimate matter, or "first timber," necessarily exists as the condition of all things, but it remains as one of those possibilities which can never be realised (see above, p. 56), and thus forms the antithesis to God, the ever-actual. From all this it may be inferred that Aristotle would have considered it very unphilosophical to represent Matter, as some philosophers of the present day appear to do, as having had an independent existence, and as having contained the germs, not only of all other things, but even of Reason itself, so that out of Matter Reason was developed. According to Aristotle, it is impossible to conceive Matter at all as actually existing, far less as the one independent antecedent cause of all things; and it is equally impossible to think of Reason as non-existent, or as having had a late and derivative origin.

Subsidiary to his theory of knowledge, Aristotle discourses at some length, both in his treatise 'On the Soul' and in his 'Physiological Tracts,' on the Five Senses. He affirms that the sentient soul of man is able to discriminate between the properties of things, "because it is itself a mean or middle term between the two sensible extremes of which it takes cognisance,—hot and cold, hard and soft, wet and dry, white and black, acute and grave, bitter and sweet, light and darkness, &c. We feel no sensation at all when the object touched is exactly of the same temperature with ourselves, neither hotter nor colder." * This doctrine, which is obviously true, points to the relativity of the qualities of things; it shows that all qualities—*e.g.*, "great" and "small," and all the rest—are named from the human stand-point, and that, in short, "Man is the measure of all things." Protagoras, indeed, had used this *dictum* in order to throw doubt on all knowledge and truth, for he said that everything was relative to the individual percipient, and that what ap-

---

* Grote's 'Aristotle,' vol. ii. p. 197. See 'On the Soul,' II. x.

peared sweet to one man might seem bitter to another man; thus, that there could be no truth beyond "what any one troweth;" any assertion might be true for the individual who made it, and not for any one besides. Aristotle argues against this sceptical theory, ('Metaphys.' III. iv.); in spite of minor fluctuations in the subjective perceptions of individuals he finds ground for truth and certainty in the *consensus* of the human race, and in science which deals with universal propositions obtained by reason out of particular perceptions.

As usual, there is a great contrast between the correctness of his general philosophy of the senses and that of his particular scientific theory of the operation of each sense. While the world has made no advance upon the one—which was arrived at by mere force of thought—the other, lacking the aid of instruments and accumulated experience, has been wholly left behind, and appears infantile when compared with the discoveries of a Helmholtz. The following is a specimen of Aristotle's physiology of the senses: "Do sensations travel to us?" he asks. "Certainly," is the reply; "the nearest person will catch an odour first. Sound is perceived *after* the blow which caused it. The letters of which words are composed get disarranged by being carried in the air (!), and hence people fail to hear what has been said at a distance. Each sense has its own proper vehicle. Water is the vehicle of sight, air of sound, fire of smell, earth of touch and taste. Sensations are not bodies, but motions or affections of the vehicle or medium along which they travel to us. Light,* however, is an exception to this rule; it is an existence, not a motion; it produces alteration, and alteration of a whole mass may be instantaneous and simultaneous, as in a mass of water freezing. Thus Empedocles was mistaken (!) when he said that light travels from the sun to the earth, and that there is a moment when each ray is not yet seen, but is being borne midway."—('Phys. Tracts.' 'On Sensation.' vi.)

Among the permanent contributions to mental science which were made by Aristotle, none is more famous than his doctrine of the "Law of Association," which he throws out while discussing Memory and Recollection in his 'Physiological Tracts.' He says, "Recollection is the recalling of knowledge. It implies the existence in the mind of certain starting-points, or clues, so that when you get hold of one you will be led to the rest. It depends on the law of association: we recollect when such and such a motion naturally follows such and such; we feel the latter motion, and that produces the former. In trying to recollect, we search after something that is in *sequence*, or *similarity*, or *contrast*, or *proximity*, to the thing which we want to recollect. Milk will suggest whiteness, whiteness the air, the air moisture, and this the rainy season, which was what we were trying to think of. No animal but man has the power of recollection, though many animals have memory. Re-

---

* The theory of light here given seems to be not only erroneous in itself, but also inconsistent with Aristotle's explanation of the twinkling of the stars.—(See above, p. 136.)

collection implies consideration and a train of reasoning, and yet it is a bodily affection—a physical movement and presentation." Aristotle adds that "persons with large heads are bad at recollecting, on account of the weight upon their perceptive organ (!), and that the very young and very old are so, on account of the state of movement they are in—the one in the movement of growth, the other in that of decay."

These considerations, however, whether correct or erroneous, all belong rather to psychology than to metaphysics. Let us conclude by endeavouring to gather Aristotle's opinions on three great metaphysical problems: The destiny of the human soul, free will, and the nature of God. His opinions on these subjects have to be "gathered," because, as said above (p. 6), he had no great taste for such speculations, and was in this respect very unlike Plato. Over the mind of Plato the idea of a future life had exercised an absorbing influence. Rising to an almost Christian hope and faith, he had held out, as a consolation in the hour of death, the promise of an immortality to be spent in the fruition of truth; and, as a motive for human actions and a basis for morals, he had enunciated a system of future rewards and punishments, closely corresponding with Heaven, Hell, and Purgatory. What had been so prominent with Plato was by Aristotle put away into the extreme background. In early life, indeed, he had written a dialogue, called 'Eudemus,' which turned on the story that an exile had been told by the oracle that within a certain time he should be "restored to his home," and that within that time he had died, and thus in another sense had "gone home." It is conjectured that this youthful production may have treated of the survival of the individual Reason into another state of existence. But in Aristotle's maturer works, so far from such a doctrine being laid down, and deductions made from it, passages occur which would seem to render it untenable. "The Soul," says Aristotle, "is the function of the body, as sight is of the eye. Some of its parts, however, may be separable from the body, as not arising out of the material organisation. This is the case with the Reason, which cannot be regarded as the result of bodily conditions, but which is divine, and enters into each of us from without. Reason, as manifested in the individual mind, is twofold, constructive and passive (see above, p. 166). The passive Reason, which receives the impressions of external things, is the seat of memory, but it perishes with the body; while the constructive Reason transcends the body, being capable of separation from it and from all things. It is an everlasting existence, incapable of being mingled with matter, or affected by it; it is prior and subsequent to the individual mind; but though immortal, it carries no memory with it." *

This last sentence would seem logically to exclude the possibility of a future life for the individual, for memory is requisite to individuality; and if all that is immortal in us is incapable of memory, it would seem that the only immortality possible would be that

* Collected from 'Soul,' II. i. 7-12; III. v. 2. 'Generation,' II. iii. 10.

of a Buddhist *nirvâna*, all the actions of this life and all individual distinctions having been erased. Thus, it would appear that the same *dictum* might be applied to the human race that is applied ('Soul,' II. iv. 4) to the works of Nature: "Perpetuity, for which all things long, is attained not by the individual, for that is impossible, but by the species." These logical deductions are, however, never drawn by Aristotle himself, who in his 'Ethics' (I. xi. 1) protests against any rude contradiction of the popular opinion that the dead retain their consciousness, and even their interest in what passes in this world. Thus, whether he did or did not believe in a future life has been a matter for controversy in modern times. On the whole, while we have hardly sufficient data for pronouncing one way or the other, it seems certain that no part of his philosophy, so far as we possess it, shows any trace of the influence of this doctrine.

As to Free Will: That is a question which has arisen out of theology, out of the ideas of the infinite power and knowledge of a personal God, which caused the question to be asked, Can man do anything except what he has been predestined to do? But such a difficulty implies two conditions, both of which were absent from the mind of Aristotle—namely, a strong apprehension of the personality and will of God, and a strong apprehension of the importance of human acts and of the eternal consequences attached to them. Aristotle, as we shall see, can hardly be said to have attributed personality to the Deity; he thought human actions to be of comparatively small importance; and he thought freedom to be, in a certain sense, valueless. Hence, we only mention the problem of Free Will in connection with him in order to show how his ideas contrast with those of the modern world. By a curious metaphor ('Metaphys.' XI. x.), he figured the universe as a household, in which the sun and stars and all the heavens are the masters, whose high aims and important positions prevent any of their time being left to a merely arbitrary disposal, for all is taken up with a round of the noblest duties and occupations. Other parts of the universe are like the inferior members of the family— the slaves and domestic animals—who can to a great extent pursue their own devices. Under the last category man would be ranked. Aristotle does not regard the unchanging and perpetual motion of the heavenly bodies as a bondage, nor what is arbitrary in the human will as a privilege. His cosmical views tended to disparage the dignity of man. He would say with the Psalmist, "What is man in comparison with the heavens?" But he failed to reach the counterbalancing thought of Kant, that "There are two things which strike the mind with awe—the starry heavens and the moral nature of man."

Within an eternal and immutable circumference of the heavens, Aristotle placed a comparatively narrow sphere of the changeable, and in this, Nature, Chance, and Human Will were the causes at work. He admitted a certain amount of determinism as controlling the human will, but he did not care to trace out the exact proportions of this; he merely maintained that the individual was a "joint cause," if not the sole cause, of his own character and actions ('Eth.' III. vii. 20). He thought that mankind had existed from all eternity, and that there had been over and over again a constant process of development going on, till the sciences, and arts, and society had been brought to perfection; and then that by some great deluge, or other natural convulsion, the race had invariably been destroyed—all but a few individuals who had escaped, and who had had to commence anew the first steps towards civilisation!

To us, in the present day, it seems absolutely clear that when we speak of a person we do not mean a thing, and that when we speak of a thing we do not mean a person. In Grecian philosophy, however, this was not the case, for by both Plato * and Aristotle, God was spoken of both as personal and as impersonal, without any reconciliation between the two points of view, or any remark on the subject. In the same way they both pass from the plural to the singular, and speak of "the gods" or "God" as if it hardly mattered which term was used. This seems at first surprising, but when we look into the matter (confining our inquiry to the views of Aristotle), certain explanations offer themselves. When he speaks of "the gods," he is partly accommodating himself to the ordinary language of Greece, and partly he is indicating the heavenly bodies, as conscious, happy

* See Professor Jowett's 'Dialogues of Plato Translated,' vol. iv. p. 11.

existences, worthy to be reckoned with that Supreme God, Who inhabits the outside of the universe, and imparts their everlasting motion to the heavens. When he speaks of "God," he has in his mind that Supreme Being, Who, unmoved Himself, is the cause of motion to all things, being the object of reason and of desire—being, in short, the Good. Here the transition from a person to an abstract idea is obvious; but if God is the object of desire to the universe and to Nature, who or what is it that desires Him? Clearly, reason or divine instinct is placed by this theory within Nature itself. In other words, this is Pantheism; it represents Nature as instinct with God, and God in Nature desiring God as the Idea of Good. But Aristotle passes on from this view to describe God as "Thought"—that is, as rather more personal than impersonal—and he asks, on what does that thought think? Thought must have an object, and it will be determined in its character by that object; it will be elevated or deteriorated according as the object on which it thinks is high or low. But this cannot be the case with God, who cannot be subject to these alterations. "God, therefore, must think upon Himself; the thought of God is the thinking upon thought." Only for a moment ('Metaphys.' XI. x. 1) does Aristotle seem to take up something like our point of view, when he says that God may be to the world as the general is to an army. This seems like the modern view, because it would imply something like will in the nature of God. But it is a mere passing metaphor, and none of the other utterances of the Stagirite would attribute anything like will, providence, or ordering of affairs to the Deity. We are told ('Eth.' X. viii. 7) that it would be absurd to attribute to Him moral qualities or virtues, or any human function except philosophic thought. He enjoys, however, happiness of the most exalted kind, such as we can frame but an indistinct notion of by the analogy of our own highest and most blessed moods. This happiness is everlasting, and God "has, or rather is," continuous and eternal life and duration.*

We have been unavoidably launched upon a solemn subject, because any account of Aristotle which did not sketch his theories of the Deity would have been incomplete. It will be seen that, on the whole, his tendency is to what we should call Pantheism. "Reason is divine, and Reason is everywhere, desiring the Good and moving the world:" that is a summary of Aristotle's philosophy. Of all modern speculators, the one who most nearly approaches him is John Stuart Mill, who represents God as benevolent, but not omnipotent. Aristotle also would say that the desire for the Good which runs through Nature is baffled by the imperfections of matter and the irregularities of chance. The great defect in Aristotle's conception of God is, that he denies that God can be a moral Being. This, in fact, entirely separates God from man; it leaves only Theology possible, but not

* The above statement of Aristotle's views of the Deity is collected from 'Metaphysics,' XI. vi.-x.

Religion; it takes away from morality all divine sanctions. Plato's view was different; but even he fell short of that deep idea of God, as the Righteous One, which was revealed to the Hebrew nation through their lawgivers and prophets, and afterwards through our Saviour.

CHAPTER X.

ARISTOTLE SINCE THE CHRISTIAN ERA.

We have seen above (p. 38) that in the time of Cicero —that is to say, shortly before the Christian era—the works of Aristotle were very little known even to philosophers. The edition of those works by Andronicus was made and published in the last half-century before the birth of Christ. And then—three hundred years after the death of Aristotle—there began silently and imperceptibly the first dawn of that wider reputation of him, which was destined to shine through the whole of Europe for a thousand years with ever-growing and increasing splendour.

During the period of the Roman Empire, the day for original philosophies was gone by. The works of Aristotle, in the form in which they were now presented to the world—being a culmination of ancient thought, and containing a dogmatic exposition of the outlines of every science; being rich in ideas and facts, precise in terms, and yet condensed, and often obscure—offered to the minds of intellectual men, and especially the subtle Greeks of those times, exactly the kind of food and employment which suited them. To study one of these treatises, and comment upon it, became now regarded as sufficient achievement for the life of one man. Aristotle thus shared the honours awarded to the sacred books of different nations; he became placed so high as an authority, that merely to expound or explain his meaning was a path to fame. The race of Greek commentators, or "Scholiasts," was spread over three or four centuries, the most distinguished names among them being those of Boethus, Nicolas of Damascus, Alexander of Ægæ, Aspasius, Adrastus, Galenus, Alexander of Aphrodisias, Porphyry, Iamblichus, Dexippus, Themistius, Proclus, Ammonius, David the Armenian, Asclepius, Olympiodorus, Simplicius, and Johannes Philoponus. The writings of many of these worthies have been lost, and their memory only survives through their having been quoted in the more enduring commentaries of others. What remains of the whole body of these *Scholia* is various in worth, ranging from emptiest platitudes up to remarks of subtlety and ability. Occasionally, but too rarely, the Greek scholiasts preserve for us some precious sentence or tradition of antiquity. The late Professor Brandis has condensed into one closely-printed quarto volume all that he considered worth notice of the "*Scholia* upon Aristotle," and even with some of these we might have dispensed.

Gradually Christianity took possession of the Roman Empire, and then came the inundation of barbarians, whose uncultivated natures had no sympathy with literature, science, or philosophy. Libraries were destroyed, or, unused, underwent the course of natural decay. The arts fell into abeyance, and Western Europe, as if in order to be born again, seemed to pass through the waters of Lethe. From the sixth to the thirteenth century all knowledge of the Greek writers was lost. But long before the close of this period intellectual life had begun to stir again among the friars and ecclesiastics of the Continent; and the chief nourishment for that life consisted of a fragment from antiquity, being none other than Latin translations* of the so-called 'Categories' and 'Interpretation' of Aristotle (see above, pp. 50-57), and of the 'Introduction' of Porphyry to the first-named of the two treatises. In earlier and better-informed ages Aristotle had been repudiated by some of the Fathers of the Church as being, at all events in comparison with Plato, "atheistical." But no harm to theology could arise from a study of the dry formulæ of logic and metaphysics. Nay, these formulæ, while totally devoid of all dangerous colouring or character—being merely some of the fundamental and ordinary principles of reasoning — were likely to do good service to the Church, by training her adherents to argue skilfully in her behalf. Thus, the 'Categories' and 'Interpretation' won their place as text-books for youth; and thus the "Scholastic Philosophy," which consisted in lectures and disputations chiefly on matters mooted by Aristotle, took its rise out of the Latin translations of these Peripatetic treatises.

Afterwards a richer knowledge of Aristotle came to the schools of the West from what might have been considered an unlikely source—namely, the Arabs in

---

* These translations were attributed to Boethius, the "last of the philosophers," at the end of the fifth and beginning of the sixth century.

Spain. Departing from the example of him who burned the Alexandrian library, and from the traditionary tendencies of Mahometans in all ages, the Arabs of Bagdad, Cairo, and Cordova indulged in a period of enlightenment and of intellectual activity. This period was chiefly inaugurated by Almamun, the son of Harun-al-Raschid, and seventh of the Abbasside Caliphs at Bagdad (A.D. 810), who "invited the Muses from their ancient seats. His ambassadors at Constantinople, his agents in Armenia, Syria, and Egypt, collected the volumes of Grecian science; at his command they were translated by the most skilful interpreters into the Arabic language; his subjects were exhorted assiduously to peruse these instructive writings; and the successor of Mahomet assisted with pleasure and modesty at the assemblies and disputations of the learned." "The age of Arabian learning continued about five hundred years till the great irruption of the Moguls, and was coeval with the darkest and most slothful period of European annals."* It was during the twelfth century that the Arabs of Cordova became the schoolmasters of the "schoolmen," and poured a flood of learning into Europe. The chief of them was the great Ibn-Raschid (A.D. 1120-1198), whose name was Latinised into Averroes. Besides other philosophical works, he wrote 'Commentaries' on all the principal works of Aristotle, and these were translated into Latin and published abroad. Averroes knew no Greek, and his commentaries were made upon the existing Arabic versions of Aristotle; but he

* Gibbon's 'Decline and Fall of the Roman Empire,' chap. lii.

quoted the translation of the text of each passage entire before elucidating the meaning, and thus he brought a great deal of the thought of Aristotle, though passed through a double translation, to the notice of Europe. In commenting upon Aristotle, his attention seems to have been drawn to that passage, above referred to (p. 172), on the difference between the Constructive and the Passive Reason. Following out this idea, he made it the basis of a doctrine of "Monopsychism," to the effect that the Constructive Reason is one individual substance, being one and the same in Socrates and Plato, and all other individuals; whence it follows that individuality consists only in bodily sensations, which are perishable, so that nothing which is individual can be immortal, and nothing which is immortal can be individual. These doctrines spread from the Arabs to the Jews of Spain, and from them to the Christian schools, and Averroism became a leaven in the scholastic philosophies, causing, as might be expected, the most virulent strife between the opponents and supporters of the theory of "Monopsychism."

In the latter part of the thirteenth century Aristotle reached the height of his glory. At this time, partly from Arabian copies in Spain and partly from Greek MSS which the Crusaders brought with them from Constantinople, Western Christendom had obtained the whole of his works. He was now commented on by eminent ecclesiastics; indeed he occupied and almost monopolised the most powerful minds of Europe. Chief among these may be mentioned Albert "the Great," the most fertile and learned of the schoolmen, who has left commentaries on Aristotle which fill six folio volumes; and his pupil, St Thomas Aquinas, who prepared (1260-70), through the instrumentality of the monk Wilhelm of Moerbecke, a new translation of the entire works after Greek originals; and who himself wrote laborious commentaries on the 'Metaphysics,' the 'Ethics,' and other books. It may be observed that by these great churchmen Aristotle is treated with the most implicit confidence; they seem blind to all that is Greek and pagan in his point of view; they defend him from charges of Averroism; and treat him, in short, as one of themselves. All this, of course, argues a great want of the critical and historical faculty, and much mixing up of things—"syncretism," as it is called by the learned; but historical criticism was hardly to be looked for in the Middle Ages.

The Stagirite was now almost incorporated with Christianity. The *Summa Theologiæ* of St Thomas Aquinas was a compound of the logic, physics, and ethics of Aristotle with Christian divinity. But the highest honour of all came to him in the year 1300 A.D., when he was hailed in the 'Divina Commedia' of Dante as "the master of those that know," sitting as head of "the philosophic family," to whom Socrates and Plato and all the rest must look up.* Him Dante

* Dante, 'Inferno,' canto iv. 131—
" Vidi il Maestro di color che sanno
Seder tra filosofica famiglia ;
Tutti lo miran, tutti onor gli fanno.
Quivi vid' io Socrate e Platone,
Che innanzi agli altri piu presso gli stanno."

figured thus sitting in the "limbo," or fringe, of hell, with all the great spirits of antiquity, who had lived before Christianity and without baptism; they were free from torment, but were sad, because they felt the desire, but had no hope, of seeing God.

Dante had been a diligent and reverential student of Aristotle, especially in the commentaries of St Thomas Aquinas. In his 'Convito,' he says that "Aristotle is most worthy of trust and obedience, as being the master-artist who considers of and teaches us the end * of human life, to which, as men, we are ordained." In the 11th canto of the 'Inferno,' he follows up Aristotle's views of the "unnatural" character of usury (see above, p. 122), and places usurers in hell among those who do violence to God and Nature, the reasons for which he sets forth in a learned discourse. But the most striking thing of all is to find that Dante, in the 24th canto of the 'Paradiso,' commences the statement of his own theological creed in words taken directly from Aristotle's definition of the Deity—

"I in one God believe;
One sole eternal Godhead, *of whose love
All heaven is moved, himself unmoved the while.*" †

And in the 27th canto, Beatrice, standing on the ninth heaven, points to the circumference, or *primum mobile*, of Aristotle (see above, p. 136), and discourses to Dante in the following thoroughly Aristotelian terms :—

---

* This, of course, refers to the 'Ethics.'—See above, p. 101.
† Cary's Translation.—See above, p. 176.

> " Here is the goal, whence motion on his race
> Starts: motionless the centre, and the rest
> All moved around. Except the soul divine,
> Place in this heaven is none; the soul divine,
> Wherein the love, which ruleth o'er its orb,
> Is kindled, and the virtue, that it sheds:
> One circle, light and love, enclasping it,
> As this doth clasp the others; and to Him,
> Who draws the bound, its limit only known.
> Measured itself by none, it doth divide
> Motion to all, counted unto them forth,
> As by the fifth or half ye count forth ten.
> The vase, wherein time's roots are plunged, thou seest:
> Look elsewhere for the leaves."

It was not till 240 years after these verses had been written that Copernicus propounded his system of the motion of the earth and the other planets round the sun; and that system only gradually won its way to acceptance, even in scientific minds, and with the aid of the demonstrations of Galileo. Till the end of the seventeenth century the Aristotelian system—further elaborated by the Alexandrian Ptolemy and by King Alphonso X. of Castile (1252-1284 A.D.)—maintained its influence, and filled the literature of all Europe with a particular train of associations.* Shakespeare lived and died in the faith of the older system. Milton had been bred in it as a boy, and the plan of his universe in the 'Paradise Lost' was drawn accord-

---

* When Shakespeare wrote—

"And certain stars shot madly from their spheres,"

he was referring to the Ptolemaic or Alphonsine spheres. The common metaphor of a person's "sphere" is a survival of the same notion.

ing to it. Yet still, as a learned man, he was well acquainted with all that could be said in favour of the Copernican system. And he puts these arguments into the mouth of Adam in the 8th book of 'Paradise Lost.' An angel, in reply, reminds Adam—what is, in fact, the case—that neither the motion of the sun nor of the earth can be absolutely proved; and adds that these are matters too high and abstruse for human inquiry. Milton's mind was "apparently uncertain to the last which of the two systems, the Ptolemaic or the Copernican, was the true one."* Surely, however, if but slowly, the Copernican theory established itself in the mind of Europe; and when once it had been established, then a great gulf was set between Aristotle and the modern world.

We have seen Aristotle an object of reverence to the great scholastic philosophers and the great poet of the Middle Ages. But we must not forget that the universities were, so to speak, founded in Aristotle —that for a long time the chief end of their being was to teach Aristotle. Chaucer describes the zeal of the poor Oxford student for this kind of learning in the following terms :—

> " A clerk there was of Oxenford also
> That unto logik hadde long y go:
> As lene was his hors as is a rake,
> And he was not right fast, I undertake ;
> But looked holwe and thereto soberlye.
> Ful threadbare was his overest courtepye.

---

* See Professor Masson's edition of 'Milton's Poetical Works' (Macmillan, 1874), vol. i. p. 92.

> For he had gotten him no benefice,
> He was not worldly to have an office.
> For, him was lever have at his beddes hed
> Twenty bookes clothed in blake or red
> Of Aristotle and his philosophie,
> Than robes rich or fidel or sautrie."

This almost living picture from the fourteenth century doubtless represented correctly the loyal and undoubting faith in the Stagirite, to be found among many generations of students, not only at Oxford, but at Paris and Padua, and the other seats of universities.

But a spirit of revolt against authority in general, and especially against the authority of Aristotle, was destined to show itself, being fostered by the progress of time, the revival of learning, and the Reformation. In the year 1536 we find Peter Ramus, then a youth of twenty years of age, choosing as the subject of his thesis for the M.A. degree, in the University of Paris, the proposition, that "Whatever has been said by Aristotle is false!" It may be imagined with what consternation the announcement of this thesis, which seemed scarcely less than blasphemous, was received by the academical authorities. However, the young Ramus acquitted himself with such ability, as well as boldness, that he obtained his degree and the licence to teach. This licence he employed in lecturing and writing against the Peripatetic logic. He propounded a method of his own in which more attention was to be paid to the *discovery* of truth. He formed a sect of Ramists, and rallied round himself the malcontent spirits of France, Germany, and Switzerland. In some of the universities Ramism obtained a firm hold. But he had to fight a hard battle with the Aristotelians, who were armed with official power, and not slow to use it in the way of persecution; his books were often condemned to be suppressed, and finally he was a martyr to the cause which he had chosen. Being a Huguenot, he was assassinated by his Aristotelian enemies during the massacre of St Bartholomew (1572 A.D.) The arguments of Ramus seem nowadays to have no weight against the 'Organon' of Aristotle, but they are valid against that perverted use of the 'Organon' which constituted the Scholastic method. It was quite necessary that the spell which Aristotle had so long exercised over the world should be broken and Ramus did good service in somewhat rudely assailing it.

If the first great attack upon Aristotle proceeded from a spirit of revolt within the logic-schools, the second was a direct manifestation of the results of the Renaissance, and consisted in bringing learning and criticism to bear upon the works of Aristotle. This was done by Patrizzi, or Patricius, who brought out his 'Discussiones Peripatcticæ' at Bâle in 1571. Patricius possessed a combination of character which is fortunately not often seen,—being extremely learned and very able, but, at the same time, ill-conditioned, egotistical, and wrong-headed. Preferring in his own mind a sort of Neo-Platonic philosophy to the Peripatetic system, he set himself to work in the book just mentioned to pull Aristotle to pieces. The first section of the 'Discussiones' treated of the life and morals of the Stagirite, and raked together against him all the personal charges to be found scattered through the remains of antiquity (see above, p. 28); the second section critically assailed with great learning the genuineness of the works of Aristotle, and proved them all to be spurious (!) The remaining sections undertook to refute the system of philosophy which they contained. The attack of Patricius was overdone in malignity, yet still it had a powerful effect in inducing men to think for themselves when they saw the claims of their oracle thus stringently called in question.

Another impulse to reaction against authority was given by science itself, in the shape of discoveries which were irreconcilable with the *dicta* of authority. In the year 1592, Galileo, wishing to test the truth of Aristotle's principle that "the velocity of falling bodies is proportionate to their weight," ascended the leaning tower of Pisa, and launching bodies of different weight, demonstrated that they reached the ground simultaneously, and thus that the principle which had been so long held with undoubting faith was erroneous. The Aristotelians of Pisa, however, were so much annoyed by this demonstration, that they compelled Galileo to leave the city.

Aristotle's philosophy had, since the days of St Thomas Aquinas, been bound up with the Catholic Church. Therefore it is not to be wondered at that Luther, in the commencement of the Reformation, should have "inveighed against the Aristotelian logic and metaphysics, or rather against the sciences themselves; nor was Melanchthon at that time much behind him. But time ripened in this, as it did in theology, the disciple's excellent understanding; and he even obtained influence enough over the master to make him retract some of that invective against philosophy which at first threatened to bear down all human reason. Melanchthon became a strenuous advocate of Aristotle, in opposition to all other ancient philosophy. He introduced into the University of Wittenberg, to which all Protestant Germany looked up, a scheme of dialectics and physics, founded upon the Peripatetic school, but improved by his own acuteness and knowledge. Thus in his books the physical science of antiquity is enlarged by all that had been added in astronomy and physiology. It need hardly be said that the authority of Scripture was always resorted to as controlling a philosophy which had been considered unfavourable to natural religion."[*] This system of Melanchthon's got the nickname of the "Philippic Method," and it was received with so much favour in the Protestant Universities of Germany as to cause these Universities to oppose the spread of Ramism.

Scholasticism and the love of authority died hard, and not without many a struggle. It is recorded that so late as the year 1629 an Act of the French Parliament was passed forbidding attacks upon Aristotle! The Jesuits employed the Peripatetic tenets in arguing against free-thinkers like Descartes. Even to the present day the manuals of philosophy in Roman Catholic ecclesiastical establishments are a *résumé* of Aristotle.

[*] Hallam's 'Introduction to the Literature of Europe.' Part I, chap. iii.

Until the seventeenth century, when the authority of Aristotle was questioned, "his disciples could always point with scorn at the endeavours which had as yet been made to supplant it, they could ask whether the wisdom so long reverenced was to be set aside for the fanatical reveries of Paracelsus, the unintelligible ideas of Bruno, or the arbitrary hypotheses of Telesio."* But in the seventeenth century modern philosophy took a new and splendid start in Bacon and Descartes, while modern science commenced its glorious career with Galileo, Kepler, and Newton. Bacon, with his rich scientific imagination and his stately language, was a fitting herald of the new era. He sometimes reflects the spirit of Ramus or Patricius, and applies to Aristotle harsh terms which were rather merited by the scholastic pedants who had been Aristotelians only in the letter. Could the Stagirite himself have returned to the earth at this moment, he would doubtless have declared for Galileo and Bacon against the Peripatetics. Aristotelianism was not refuted in Europe, but its long day was now past; it was superseded and quietly put aside when other and fresher subjects of interest came to fill men's minds. Bacon contributed to this result, not by railing at the "categories" and the "syllogism," but by exciting people's fancy with suggestions of the extension of human power to be gained by researches into nature—suggestions which subsequent results have verified a hundred-fold.

From henceforth it became impossible for an educated man to be an Aristotelian, because however much he

* Hallam's Introduction. Part III., chap. iii.

might in his youth have learned from Aristotle, there was so much more to be learned which was not to be found in Aristotle, that Aristotelianism could only constitute a portion of his culture. In the Middle Ages it had constituted the whole of culture; but that time had gone by, and in the modern world it became possible to gain elsewhere even most of that which the study of Aristotle had to offer. The best of Aristotle's thought had now come to be the common property of the world, and men could become good logicians without reading the 'Organon,' and without being conscious of the obligations which, after all, they owed to its author.

Perhaps the period of the greatest neglect which the memory of Aristotle underwent since the Christian era was the eighteenth century. This was a period of antithesis to mediævalism, and, at the same time, a period of mechanical philosophy and shallow learning. At the English universities all studies, except perhaps mathematics and verbal scholarship, were at a low ebb. Only small portions of Aristotle were taught, and these were ill taught without reference to their context and real significance. But with the nineteenth century there came a restitution of the honours of the Stagirite, who was now regarded in his proper light— that is to say, historically, and not as if he were an authority for modern times. This came about with the rise of the great German philosophies. There have been two great periods of philosophy in the world: the period of Greek philosophy in the 5th and 4th centuries B.C., and that of German philosophy during the first part of the present century. And there is a certain affinity between the two. Kant and Hegel have more in common with Plato and Aristotle than they have either with the scholastic philosophy or with the psychological systems of the last century. An age which produced Kant and Hegel was likely to appreciate their ancient forerunners; and Hegel advocated the study of the works of Aristotle as "the noblest problem of classical philology." The Germans have applied themselves to this problem with splendid success, especially Immanuel Bekker, Brandis, Zeller, Bonitz, Spengel, Stahr, Bernays, Rose, and many others who might be mentioned. The great Berlin edition of the works of Aristotle, brought out under the auspices of the Prussian Royal Academy, is a monument of their labours. We have seen the vicissitudes of reputation through which Aristotle has passed —how at different times he was partially known, misconceived, over-rated, under-rated, and both praised and blamed on wrong grounds. Perhaps at no previous time has he been more correctly known and estimated than he is at present.

The various services of Aristotle to mankind have been to some extent indicated in the foregoing pages. To attempt to summarise them all would be vain; but perhaps it may be said, in a word, that Aristotle has contributed more than any one man to the scientific education of the world. The amount of the influence which he has exercised may partly be inferred from the traces which his system has left in all the languages of modern Europe. Our everyday conversation is full of Aristotelian "fossils," that is, remnants of his peculiar phraseology. These mostly come through Latin renderings of his terms, though sometimes the original Greek form is preserved. The following are a few specimens of these fossils: "Maxim" is the major premiss of the Aristotelian syllogism. "Principle" has the same meaning—it comes from *principium*, the Latin for "beginning" or "starting-point," which was one of Aristotle's terms for a major premiss. "Matter" comes from *materies*, the Latin for "timber" (see above, p. 167); when we say "it does not matter," or it makes a "material" difference, we are indebted to Aristotle for our words. "Form," "end," "final cause," "motive," "energy," "actually," "category," "predicament" (the latter of these two being Latin for the former), the "mean" and the "extremes," "habit" (both in the sense of "moral habit" and of "dress"), "faculty," and "quintessence," are all purely Peripatetic; while the terms "Metaphysics" and "Natural History," are derived from two of the titles of Aristotle's works.

Aristotle, the strongest of the ancients and the oracle of the Middle Ages, must always hold a place of honour in the history of European thought. Writings which have interested and influenced mankind so deeply and through so many centuries can never fall into contempt, even though they may be devoid of the graces of style and though the matter in them may be either superseded or else absorbed into the treatises of other authors. Nor is it from mere curiosity—from a merely antiquarian or historical point of view—that the works of the Stagirite continue to be studied. As long as the process of higher education in modern Europe consists so largely in imbuing the mind with the literature of classical antiquity, so long will a study of certain works of Aristotle remain as one of the last stages of that process. Those works—especially the 'Rhetoric,' 'Art of Poetry,' 'Ethics,' and 'Politics'—have a remarkable educational value. They form an introduction to philosophy; they invite comparison of ancient and modern ways of thinking; they offer rich stores of information as to human nature—so much the same in all ages; and they train the mind to follow the Aristotelian method of analytic insight. This method consists in concentration of the mind upon the subject in hand, marshalling together all the facts and opinions attainable upon it, and dwelling on these and scrutinising and comparing them till a light flashes on the whole subject. Such is the procedure to be learnt, by imitation, from Aristotle.

END OF ARISTOTLE.

PRINTED BY WILLIAM BLACKWOOD AND SONS.

www.ingramcontent.com/pod-product-compliance
Lightning Source LLC
Chambersburg PA
CBHW020924230426
43666CB00008B/1560